Not what you expected?
Read on to give your meetings unexpected impact.

Praise for *Meet with Impact*

'I like to focus on getting outcomes through high-quality conversations and diverse ways of working. This book has oodles of practical tips for everyone, no matter what their experience and role, and I'd commend it to anyone who knows that people make better decisions when they work well together.'

Adrinne Kelbie, CEO, Office for Nuclear Regulation

'Competitive advantage is the holy grail of all companies today, but how do you achieve it? One of the most effective and sustainable ways is through your people. If you can inspire, motivate and energise your people around the collective success of the organisation magic can happen. Using the principles described in this book you can meet and impact your employees, customers and investors and achieve competitive advantage and create a better future for your organisation. It all starts with making meetings deliver your desired outcomes. I have had the privilege of working with Tom Russell and many occasions in many different settings and I have seen first-hand this transformation take place with the groups he has worked with. I highly recommend Tom's work and the ideas, principles and methodology Tom has shared in this remarkable book.'

David Ednie, President and CEO, SalesChannel International

'This is a book that makes you question why and how you have meetings. It brings a new energy to a concept that has got stale in many organisations. If you take on board these tips, hints and advice I am sure that your meetings will drive better decisions, save time and be a far more fun experience!'

Andy Rogers, Global HR Director, Sodexo Government

'This book is a compelling and insightful resource to help you achieve more productive meetings and to give energy and momentum to the actions that follow – use it and enjoy the results!'

Monika Vikander-Hegarty, Vice President HR International and Global Talent, Teleflex

MEET WITH IMPACT

Pearson

At Pearson, we have a simple mission: to help people make more of their lives through learning.

We combine innovative learning technology with trusted content and educational expertise to provide engaging and effective learning experiences that serve people wherever and whenever they are learning.

From classroom to boardroom, our curriculum materials, digital learning tools and testing programmes help to educate millions of people worldwide – more than any other private enterprise.

Every day our work helps learning flourish, and wherever learning flourishes, so do people.

To learn more, please visit us at **www.pearson.com/uk**

MEET WITH IMPACT

40 VISUAL TOOLS FOR PRODUCTIVE MEETINGS AND ENGAGING WORKSHOPS

TOM RUSSELL

Pearson

Harlow, England • London • New York • Boston • San Francisco • Toronto • Sydney • Dubai • Singapore • Hong Kong
Tokyo • Seoul • Taipei • New Delhi • Cape Town • São Paulo • Mexico City • Madrid • Amsterdam • Munich • Paris • Milan

PEARSON EDUCATION LIMITED
KAO Two
KAO Park
Harlow CM17 9SR
United Kingdom
Tel: +44 (0)1279 623623
Web: www.pearson.com/uk

First edition published 2019 (print and electronic)

ISBN: 978-1-292-26295-6 (print)
        978-1-292-26296-3 (PDF)
        978-1-292-26297-0 (ePub)

British Library Cataloguing-in-Publication Data
A catalogue record for the print edition is available from the British Library

Library of Congress Cataloging-in-Publication Data
A catalog record for the print edition is available from the Library of Congress

10 9 8 7 6 5 4 3 2 1
23 22 21 20 19

Cover design by Two Associates

Print edition typeset in 9.5/14 pt Helvetica Neue LT Pro by SPi Global
Printed by Ashford Colour Press Ltd, Gosport

NOTE THAT ANY PAGE CROSS REFERENCES REFER
TO THE PRINT EDITION

For Esther, Oliver, Esme and Annabel. Also to my parents, Michael and Sylvia Russell, who have been my visual inspiration right from the moment I was tall enough to pinch their pens and paper from the desk in the studio.

CONTENTS

Acknowledgements xvi

Publisher's acknowledgements xvii

About the author xviii

About the illustrator xix

SECTION 1 - ADVENTURES IN THE LAND OF MEETINGS – BEING TOGETHER REALLY IS BETTER

- Format and framing 3
- We need meetings 6
- What are you and your organisation experiencing? 7
- Reasons to be cheerful 8
- Why 'impact'? 9
- Change can start anywhere, with anyone, with you 10
- The tanker will turn 12

- Take your shirt off and dance! 13
- Sweat the small stuff 14
- Make the difference visible 15
- Seek forgiveness, not permission 16
- This is a knowledge share 16
- Better together 18
- The golden nuggets 19

SECTION 2 - WHY WORKING VISUALLY IS A NO-BRAINER – SIDESTEPPING MAVERICKS, HOARDERS AND HAMMERS

- Meeting Scenario 1 22
- Meeting Scenario 2 23
- The four BIG reasons why you should work visually 25
- Where have we come from? 30
- Information is good for you 31
- Information is social 32
- Understanding information 34
- Meeting culture 36
- How can I make a change? 38
- Think participant 43
- Your organisation's meeting culture 44
- The golden nuggets 46

SECTION 3 - TIN KALEIDOSCOPES AND THE TYRANNY OF URGENCY – TWO MODELS TO HELP YOU ACE YOUR MEETINGS

- Tin kaleidoscopes 48
- Purpose 50
- Content 57
- People 58
- People and visual information 64
- Process 66
- The tyranny of urgency 68
- The five stages of a successful meeting 73
- The golden nuggets 75

SECTION 4 - VIRTUAL, VISUAL AND VIRTUOUS – MAKING AN IMPACT EVEN WHEN THERE'S NO MEETING ROOM

- The legacy of Eyjafjallajökull 78
- Virtual meetings – the good, the bad and the ugly 81
- Agreeing ways of working 92
- Capturing ways of working 93
- Getting visual with the virtual 94
- 10 tips to be more effective – virtually 95
- It's OK to break away 99
- The golden nuggets 100

SECTION 5 - NERDY NIBS AND CIRCULAR NIGHTMARES – GET TOOLED UP AND PLAN FOR SUCCESS

- You, the visual meeting designer 102
- What's in your toolkit? 103
- The need-to-haves 104
- The nice-to-haves 107
- Get to know your pen friend 108
- Use of colour 111
- Simple fonts 112
- Drawing bullets 113
- Simple shapes 114
- Writing text in the moment 115
- A note about the person who writes nicely 118
- Preparation preparation preparation (not 'waff waff waff') 119
- Reflecting on the deck 120
- No parking 122
- Are you bored with the board table? 123
- The golden nuggets 124

SECTION 6 - MAKING IMPACT HAPPEN – 40 ESSENTIAL VISUAL TOOLS THAT BELONG TO YOU

- How the tools are organised 126
- Meet the experts 129
- It's not what you do, it's the way that you do it 129
- The Meet with Impact Planner 130
- Using the Meet with Impact Planner 130
- The tools! 136

SECTION 7 - WHAT JUST HAPPENED? EVEN MEETING SUPERHEROES NEED TO REFLECT

- Take time to reflect 326
- The Meet with Impact Reflection Tool 328

Your free Meet with Impact Planner and Reflection Tool 333
Sources/Bibliography 335
Index 337

ACKNOWLEDGEMENTS

A huge thank you to the following people who have made this book a reality. Firstly to Esther, for everything. To Helen Chapman, Catherine Hennessy and Ben Robinson at The Facilitation Partnership (TFP) and Inky Thinking for being an inspiration and source of unending encouragement. To Ellie Chapman for illustrating this book so wonderfully. To Jan Bovelander, David Ednie, Zelda Gray, Adriènne Kelbie, Stephen Parker, Andy Rogers, Varik Torsteinsen and Monika Vikander-Hegarty for cheering the book on. To Eloise Cook at Pearson Education for her encouragement and immense patience. To everyone who has offered their support and guidance, however small, along the way. Finally, to the numerous thinkers and doers who have inspired me in the field of meeting leadership and facilitation, thank you.

PUBLISHER'S ACKNOWLEDGEMENTS

Text credits:

006 Harvard Business Publishing: Harvard Business Review 'Stop the meeting madness', July/August 2017 **014 Hodder & Stoughton Ltd:** Black Box Thinking: Marginal Gains and the Secrets of High Performance. Matthew Syed. 2016. John Murray. **017 Oxford University Press:** The Knowledge Creating Company: How Japanese Companies Create the Dynamics of Innovation. Iku-jiro Nonaka & Hirotaka Takeuchi. 1995. Oxford University Press. **018 The Facilitation Partnership:** The Facilitation Partnership, 2016 **027 Sussex Publishers, LLC:** A New Look at Visual Thinking,' Psychology Today 2016 **033 Harvard Business Publishing:** The Social Life of Information. John Seely Brown and Paul Duguid. 2017. Harvard Business Review Press. **035 Harvard Business Publishing:** The Social Life of Information. John Seely Brown and Paul Duguid. 2017. Harvard Business Review Press. **061 Harvard Business Publishing:** The Medici Effect: What Elephants and Epidemics Can Teach Us About Innovation. Frans Johannsson. 2017. Harvard Business Review Press. **071 John Wiley & Sons:** The Facilitator's Guide to Participatory Decision Making. Sam Kaner. 2007. Jossey- Bass. **072 John Wiley & Sons:** The Facilitator's Guide to Participatory Decision Making. Sam Kaner. 2007. Jossey- Bass. **080 Gartner, Inc:** "Out of the Ashes: Business Continuity Management Lessons From Iceland's Volcanic Eruption" Gartner. 23 April 2010 **081 Pure Strategic Media Ltd:** Virtual working – is it possible to be truly engaged? HRDirector.com.2018 **119 The Facilitation Partnership:** The Facilitation Partnership, 2018.

Photo credits:

All other images/illustration/cartoons @ Ellie Chapman.

ABOUT THE AUTHOR

Tom Russell

Tom is a Co-Founder and Director of The Facilitation Partnership Limited (TFP) and Inky Thinking. Tom studied Organisational Behaviour in London before entering the Human Resources profession for organisations including Safeway Stores, Volvo Cars and Cancer Research UK. Although he has facilitated for a large part of his working life Tom formally started his facilitation career in 2010, before forming TFP and Inky Thinking with his business partners Ben, Catherine and Helen in 2013. Tom's business partners call him 'ambidextrous', meaning that he is equally comfortable facilitating or graphic recording. When he is not facilitating Tom enjoys time with his family, running, art, reading and chocolate. Tom lives in beautiful Northumberland with his wife Esther and three teenage children. Tom is a Fellow of the Royal Society of Arts (RSA).

You can contact Tom at tom@thefacilitationpartnership.com and tom@inkythinking.com

www.thefacilitationpartnership.com
www.inkythinking.com

ABOUT THE ILLUSTRATOR

Ellie Chapman

Ellie studied Interior Design before discovering the power of pen and ink. She is now drawing her way around the world with Inky Thinking. Based in London, Ellie creates graphics for clients across a range of sectors and with groups of all sizes, from large conferences to small leadership teams. Ellie brings conversations to life in graphic form to help those involved literally see what they mean. The result is a set of visual representations and tools that can be used to follow up commitments made during discussion. Ellie can also be found developing graphic animations aimed at communicating across global organisations. When she's not drawing, Ellie bakes the best cheesecake in town and compensates for her sweet tooth by running and road cycling.

You can contact Ellie at ellie@inkythinking.com

ADVENTURES IN THE LAND OF MEETINGS – BEING TOGETHER REALLY IS BETTER

When I was a child I used to own a particular book that I would read and read and never get tired of.

If I were to describe it to you I would call it a fictional adventure book. Like most books one would start at the beginning with a scene in a mystery kingdom, but that is where the similarity to a normal fictional story would end. What I loved about this book was that one could interact with the story and choose how the story would develop based on decisions I, as the reader, would make.

For example, at the beginning of the story I might find myself in a dark forest, listening to the sounds of the wildlife in the darkness. Suddenly, two paths through the trees were revealed by the moonlight – which one would I choose? If I chose the first path I would need to turn to page 20 (for example) and continue reading, but if I chose the second path I must turn to page 56, and so on.

The story would continue in this way, and I would be faced with decisions at each point in the book. Whether to fight or run, to solve a puzzle or answer a question. It was an exciting read, and no two adventures through the book appeared to be the same.

You are probably wondering why I have started writing a book about meetings describing a children's book I read years ago. Please humour me for a little longer.

FORMAT AND FRAMING

Firstly, it was the format of the book, rather than the story, that truly captured my attention. I don't remember the story, other than it was a form of fantasy adventure, but it was the opportunity to shape and direct the story through my own decisions that really attracted me.

Back then when I was a boy I wouldn't have imagined that I would be writing this book about meetings, but life is a series of choices (however big and small) and so are your meetings. If you are running meetings on a regular basis in your job or for your organisation you will know that every decision you make as meeting leader, however small, has an impact on the group's behaviour, interaction with each other, and the outcome of the meeting. This book is about choices, and my aim is to provide you with an understanding of the visual choices you can make when planning and running your meetings.

The second reason for describing this book to you is about framing. Framing in meetings is the way one provides context to a group as an introduction to a discussion or activity on a specific topic. It is about choosing one's words very carefully so that your meeting participants clearly understand what's about to happen. In essence you are providing (some even say inoculating) them with a 'snapshot of reality' with which to stimulate their thinking and conversation.

This is one of the characteristics of the children's book I particularly enjoyed, that at each point the context was carefully framed, allowing me to understand what was happening and make a decision to act. The frame set my view of the situation at hand in the context of the overall adventure.

Here are two possible sets of frames you might use to describe meetings in your organisation. Firstly, consider these comments. . .

'We all have our own opinion and there's very little agreement'

'We have so much information to work through '

'Things change, and we need to discuss again and again'

'We have to make lots of difficult decisions'

'Everyone wants to have their say all the time'

'We spend too much of our time in meetings'

What messages are you receiving? My guess is that whoever is saying this might be frustrated about their meetings and how complex they are. Maybe you can identify with them yourself? Now consider the following comments. . .

Do you notice the difference? Both sets of comments are similar; however the second group of comments are framed positively and objectively, with meetings seen as an opportunity to be embraced rather than feared.

WE NEED MEETINGS

Over the past 10 years what has struck me about meetings in many organisations is that they make a HUGE impact on our working lives. This might not be news to you, but it's true that we generally measure the impact of meetings in terms of time spent rather than other measures, such as what we achieved in them, and this all seems rather one dimensional.

> 'Meetings have increased in length and frequency over the past 50 years, to the point where executives spend an average of nearly 23 hours a week in them, up from less than 10 hours in the 1960s.
> And that doesn't even include all the impromptu gatherings that don't make it onto the schedule.'
>
> Harvard Business Review
> 'Stop the meeting madness'. July/August 2017

Meetings are collaborative, relationship building and strengthening opportunities, packed full of topics ripe for discussion and exploration. The expectations we place on our meetings should be high, and rightly so because our time together is precious. Meetings are spaces to make decisions and commitments, and a place to springboard into tangible action leading to positive results. After all, why would we need to meet if everything in life stayed the same?

WHAT ARE YOU AND YOUR ORGANISATION EXPERIENCING?

I am positive there will be other environmental influences I might have missed that you can suggest or note below. It is no surprise that many organisations feel the pressure of operating in an ever-changing environment. These pressures are often characterised in an organisation's culture, reflecting attitudes to the environment and the behaviours developed in order to remain effective, or at least that's the ideal.

Later in the book I refer to 'meeting culture', where the way an organisation holds its meetings reflects the prevailing culture within the wider business. Maybe you can already describe your organisation's meeting culture, and how this may be affected by the global context above.

So here I am, writing this book for people, like yourself, who regularly plan and lead meetings. I intend to explain to you why this book is important, and why as a meeting leader you should use your valuable time to read it.

REASONS TO BE CHEERFUL

When I am asked to describe what I do for a living I often find that people are surprised I spend so much of my time immersed in meetings. 'Who would want to do that?' is a common response, 'The meetings in my organisation are so frustrating!' 'Why not?' I say. 'What a fantastic chance to help the world to work smarter!' It's true: we – you and I – have a HUGE opportunity to demonstrate what can be achieved in our meetings every day.

Therefore, I invite you to take a wholly positive frame as you progress through this book. View what you may initially consider to be challenges as exciting opportunities to embrace. Why? Here are a few reasons why you should. . .

- You will be a more confident meeting leader.
- You will develop a reputation as someone who leads productive meetings.
- Decisions made will be more robust, with tangible impact.
- Colleagues will understand each other more deeply than before.
- Your organisation will become more effective and successful.
- The world will become a smarter place in which to work and live.

WHY 'IMPACT'?

This book is about impact. The impact you can demonstrate as a meeting leader, and the impact your meetings will have within your organisation. More specifically this book is about making a visual impact in your meetings in service of enhancing the engagement of your meeting participants and ultimately greater levels of productivity.

I've taken the liberty of assuming that you will have led a meeting before, or at least taken part in organising and making it happen. This valuable experience means that you will understand some of the situations we experience in meetings, you will recognise some of the characters I describe along the way, and you will see why the practical steps I recommend will make a smart difference in your meetings.

When you 'meet with impact' great things will happen. Likewise, if you are the impact that makes your meetings a success then others will want to meet with you to get work done.

Let's explore what impact means. Here's a basic definition of impact both as a noun and as a verb.

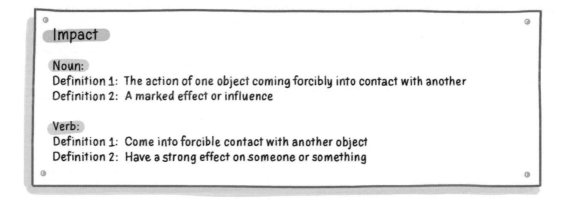

Impact

Noun:
Definition 1: The action of one object coming forcibly into contact with another
Definition 2: A marked effect or influence

Verb:
Definition 1: Come into forcible contact with another object
Definition 2: Have a strong effect on someone or something

Which definition do you prefer? You may be reading these definitions and find yourself thinking that Definition 1 both as a noun and as a verb describes the meetings in your organisation, maybe where people come together and decisions are reached predominantly through position, power and personality rather than knowledge and expertise.

Take a look at Definition 2, again as a noun and as a verb. What do you notice? Clearly there is energy in these definitions. Both are constructive and describe what could be a highly productive meeting where rich dialogue and constructive challenge lead to implemented actions and strong commitment.

That's my point: all meetings can make the impact that will help organisations to thrive. How can you make that happen? Here are a few ideas to start. . .

CHANGE CAN START ANYWHERE, WITH ANYONE, WITH YOU

Absolutely anyone can make a change to the way meetings are run in an organisation. Think of your organisation as a human being. How would you describe them? What characteristics do they exhibit? What habits, good or bad, do they have? I've left a space below for you to note their main characteristics.

- The characteristics of my organisation...

Organisations have habit-forming tendencies. Like human beings they will quickly spot a good thing and attempt to exploit it, rather like that hugely satisfying itch one can't resist even if at the outset it may have been perceived as an irritation. This applies to absolutely anything. Take e-mail for example. When it was introduced into many organisations in the 1990s it was alien, uncomfortable and difficult to understand. Remember the memo? Its fans were reluctant to let go. The rest is history.

So, if you are determined to change the way your organisation runs its meetings, then you can – you just need to help it develop the habit.

THE TANKER WILL TURN

The size of organisations can often cause many working within them to doubt whether change will or could happen. This is entirely understandable. The global environment leads to many businesses acquiring others, gradually getting bigger or growing as a result of their own success. However growth happens it often leads to bigger teams, greater infrastructure, more sophisticated communication systems and complex organisation design – the proverbial 'organisational oil tanker'. In case you're not familiar with the oil tanker analogy, the point is that it can take a fully loaded oil tanker a long time to change course or to stop, due to its weight and size.

But size doesn't mean an organisation cannot change its habits and behaviours. It only takes one small noticeable change for the better to be noticed, and change will happen. Small organisations are not immune either. Although typically more agile than their larger cousins it can be challenging to change habits especially when the vast majority of time is spent doing business rather than thinking about the business itself.

TAKE YOUR SHIRT OFF AND DANCE!

If you've not heard of the lone shirtless dancing guy you've missed a treat. Grab your phone or tablet and take a moment to look him up. He's certainly fun to watch and, as you will see, it's not the lone shirtless dancing guy who makes the biggest difference when inspiring others to change their behaviour, it's the people who follow him first (known as 'first followers'). If you could be the lone shirtless dancing guy in your meetings who will you inspire to follow you?

(Please note I am not literally proposing you take your shirt off and dance in your meetings. Of course be my guest if that's what you want to do, but please bear in mind that it could be slightly career limiting, although you will probably be the topic of conversation for months to come.)

SWEAT THE SMALL STUFF

You may be familiar with the story behind the success of Team Sky, the British Professional Cycling Team, and the approach led by Dave Brailsford. In summary, Brailsford was adamant that every tiny aspect of the team's performance, from the bikes to breakfast, could have a breakthrough impact on the team's success and making small incremental changes to these different elements could mean the difference between a medal position or going home empty handed.

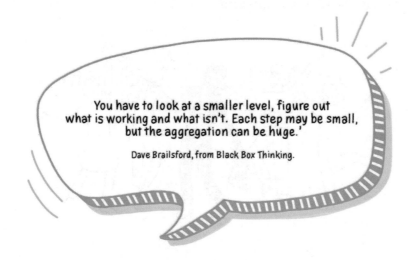

You have to look at a smaller level, figure out what is working and what isn't. Each step may be small, but the aggregation can be huge.'

Dave Brailsford, from Black Box Thinking.

Igniting change successfully in any organisation does not need to be a huge endeavour. It can start with the small things which are easier to implement, make a tangible impact, whilst allowing us to do the job we're hired to do. The notion of small actions will return later in this book, when I will introduce you to the Meeting Kaleidoscope which describes how you can successfully plan and lead your meetings by paying attention to small details.

MAKE THE DIFFERENCE VISIBLE

When implementing a tangible change, make it visible. This may sound rather obvious but really, make sure everyone can see it, because if they can see the change that has been made it will be easier to understand the benefit that change brings.

Later in the book I will introduce you to the 'PREP' tool (Tool 2). Watch out for it. This is a simple visual tool and, if you were to make only one change in your meetings, I wholeheartedly recommend you start with this one. You won't regret it.

SEEK FORGIVENESS, NOT PERMISSION

Please don't wait to be asked to make a change for the better, go ahead and do it. It's much easier to seek forgiveness than to ask for permission when you have done something that makes a positive impact on your workplace. In any case I give you permission, so you have that in the bank already. Win win!

THIS IS A KNOWLEDGE SHARE

Earlier in this section I referred to framing, and the importance of framing in meetings to focus participants on what needs to be done and why. Here's another positive frame you can use in your organisation – meetings are opportunities to build and share knowledge, thereby making organisations stronger and more effective.

In their book Nonaka and Takeuchi provide a compelling account of how Japanese organisations have focussed on the creation of knowledge for competitive advantage.

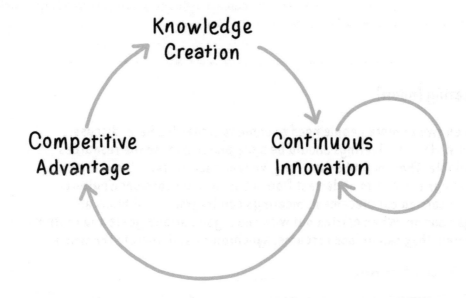

Adapted from Nonaka and Takeuchi, 1995

How does this happen? It is the conversion of tacit knowledge (which we hold in our heads) to explicit knowledge (which can be shared with others) that is at the core of knowledge creation. If we apply a mindset that our meetings present an opportunity to convert tacit to explicit knowledge, and if we are able to share and build that knowledge visually within well-designed and facilitated meetings, we are in a strong place to achieve powerful results.

BETTER TOGETHER

Before we continue into the rest of the book, let's not forget that the context of this book is meetings, in organisations large and small. Whatever the business, sector or location, a meeting can be defined as follows:

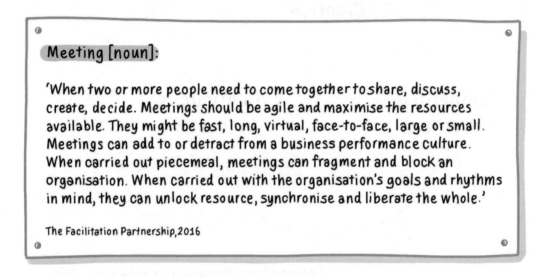

Meeting [noun]:

'When two or more people need to come together to share, discuss, create, decide. Meetings should be agile and maximise the resources available. They might be fast, long, virtual, face-to-face, large or small. Meetings can add to or detract from a business performance culture. When carried out piecemeal, meetings can fragment and block an organisation. When carried out with the organisation's goals and rhythms in mind, they can unlock resource, synchronise and liberate the whole.'

The Facilitation Partnership, 2016

The inspiration I draw from this definition is that great things happen when we come together, share knowledge, generate meaning and make powerful decisions together. The next time you prepare to plan your meeting, frame your approach with a 'better together' mindset and you will be off to an amazing start.

Below I have outlined the key points that I believe are worth remembering from this section of the book. I call these the golden nuggets, and you will find these nuggets at the end of Sections 1 to 5, in addition to an extra space to note your own nuggets.

THE GOLDEN NUGGETS

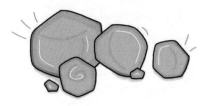

- Meetings are collaborative, relationship building and strengthening opportunities.
- Change starts with you – are you ready to make your organisation and the world work smarter?
- Your first followers are critical both to you and to change in your organisation.
- Small, visible and tangible actions are often more powerful when aiming for lasting change.
- Seek forgiveness, not permission, when making your meetings more effective.
- When you meet with impact, great things can happen.

Add your own golden nuggets, insights and inspiration here. . .

WHY WORKING VISUALLY IS A NO-BRAINER – SIDESTEPPING MAVERICKS, HOARDERS AND HAMMERS

In Section 1 we explored the challenges of meetings, and what we can all do in our organisations to make a change for the better. In this section we explore more deeply the theme of visual information, how you can use it within the meeting context and why it's useful. We also meet some of the characters you might typically work with and how they might affect your organisation's meeting culture.

In order to understand the benefits more closely, I'd like you to consider the two meeting scenarios:

MEETING SCENARIO 1

Imagine you work in a well-known clothing company. You and your colleagues are seated around a boardroom table in a bland room. There are 20 people around this long table, with the chairperson at the end. Each person in the meeting represents a different department within the business, including Finance, HR, IT, Manufacturing, Sales and so on. You are representing New Product Development (NPD).

The subject under discussion is a new line that it is hoped will hit the shops and online next year. The purpose of the meeting is to suggest ideas to the CEO, whose PA is noting the ideas down in order to decide upon the final concept. One by one, everyone around the table has a chance to suggest an idea they think the CEO will like, at which point a decision will be made outside the meeting and communicated to the group by e-mail so that implementation plans can be drafted. The meeting closes promptly once everyone has had their opportunity to suggest an idea.

MEETING SCENARIO 2

You are in a different meeting room to discuss the same subject. The room is spacious and light, there are no tables, just chairs, and lots of blank paper on the walls, and examples of clothing from your own company as well as the competition. The group has been split into smaller groups made up of mixed functional teams, and each group has a chance to generate and build on ideas using materials including sticky notes, markers and the large charts. Posters are displayed around the room showing data about market trends, as well as catalogues and industry publications.

In this meeting any suggestion is valid, leading to lots of rich ideas which are captured visually and clustered within each group into the top three ideas. Everyone contributes and has a chance to see and hear each other's ideas. Finally, each participant has an opportunity to vote for the top three ideas based on objective criteria.

Whilst it may appear obvious, let's explore what's wrong with Meeting 1, and what works in Meeting 2. . .

● Meeting 1	● Meeting 2
• The ideas offered are believed to be what the CEO wants to hear	• The ideas offered are free from judgement. No idea is invalid
• The ideas are not captured visibly, and so cannot be compared easily	• The entire thought process for each idea is made visible through the use of charts and materials
• The decision is made by one person	• The decision is made by the group, who collectively owns the outcome
• Individual strengths and opinions are less important (than the CEO)	• Everyone's unique perspective is respected and celebrated
• The meeting environment does not enable free thinking and dialogue	• The space is well thought through with obstructions removed to foster collaboration

Which meeting would you prefer to take part in? Everyone from the first meeting could quite easily take part in the second meeting, including the CEO. It goes without saying that the process of the second meeting would need to be designed well (as charts and markers alone don't equal breakthrough results). The point is that well-designed meetings that include carefully chosen visual tools lead to much greater levels of participant engagement, and subsequently better, smarter outcomes.

I've exaggerated the scenarios somewhat to make a point here, as one would hope there are no meetings taking place like that in the first scenario, but in both cases the remedy is to be aware of the choices available and to choose well.

THE FOUR BIG REASONS WHY YOU SHOULD WORK VISUALLY

1. We're already wired to think visually

I have met many meeting participants who claim not to be visual thinkers, possibly because they doubt their artistic skill or appreciation; however they have understood and willingly immersed themselves in visual techniques and processes to great effect.

It is claimed that between 65% and 80% of people are able to easily interpret, learn and generate meaning from pictures and images (Seyens Education Institute. 'Humans are visual creatures'. 2016). Whether you agree with these claims or not, what is crystal clear in my experience is that everyone, to varying degrees, has the ability to interpret, work with and benefit from visual information in meetings.

2. Engagement and participation

There is a common expression 'time flies when you're having fun'. I sincerely hope there will be meetings you can apply this sentiment to, because those are likely to be the meetings which are the most productive.

It is a fact that working visually, where participants are involved and engaged in the process of sharing and working with each other's inputs, is significantly more productive than sitting around a table in discussion or viewing a long slide deck (e.g., PowerPoint). Undoubtedly table discussions and slide decks have their place, but if you really want to get people to take ownership of their thinking and get them making decisions that truly stick then a visual process to help them actually see what they are wanting to achieve will be immensely powerful.

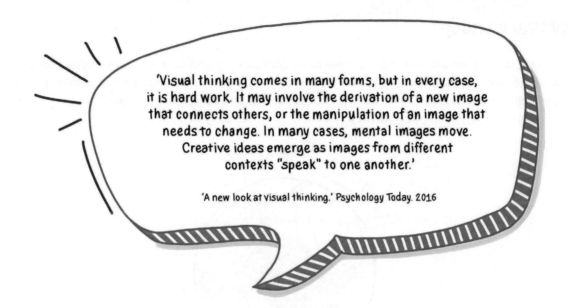

'Visual thinking comes in many forms, but in every case, it is hard work. It may involve the derivation of a new image that connects others, or the manipulation of an image that needs to change. In many cases, mental images move. Creative ideas emerge as images from different contexts "speak" to one another.'

'A new look at visual thinking.' Psychology Today. 2016

What's more, visual information often enables participants to anticipate what is coming. For example, if you are participating in a meeting and you see a flipchart split into five sections under the heading 'Business Strategies', you are likely to expect one aim of the meeting to be the creation of five strategies for the business. It's a simple point, but powerful as a support to you in your role as a meeting leader, and to aid participant expectations.

3. Cross-cultural working

Working cross-culturally is not limited to working with colleagues from other countries, but in fact includes being aware of cultural differences between organisations, departments and teams. For example, the best meetings I have led include strong process thinkers from Finance, Manufacturing and Supply Chain, working alongside 'looser' creative thinkers from Marketing, Design and NPD. All perspectives are equally valuable and to be celebrated.

The organisation in which you work will have its own distinct culture, just as all businesses will have their own 'way of doing things around here'. Acquisitive businesses regularly face challenges when employees from different business units come together in the context of transition, and working visually brings people together around an explicit focal point, signposting what's common and shared as a strong 'push-off point'.

4. Commitment and action

The visible nature of the tools described in Section 6 will help motivate meeting participants to commit to taking action after the meeting. The proliferation of mobile devices with high quality cameras means that taking photos of the work done, like taking selfies, and e-mailing them in the moment is common place.

Meeting participants should emerge from the discussion with the enthusiasm to make agreed actions a reality **AND** an instant visual record of the meeting outputs. Gone are the days when one would wait hours or days for the meeting minutes to arrive. This can now be done whilst the seats (actual or virtual) in the meeting room are still warm.

WHERE HAVE WE COME FROM?

You may not immediately think of the history that has contributed to how we communicate visually in meetings; nonetheless there is a rich tapestry of events that have led us to where we are now. Core to all these developments has been the need to communicate a message in a way that engages those receiving it, in the spirit of enriching understanding and knowledge.

Undoubtedly a number of these milestones are more significant than others, and I have added several for fun. I invite you to reflect on my interpretation and, if you think I have missed a key milestone, please add it to the timeline.

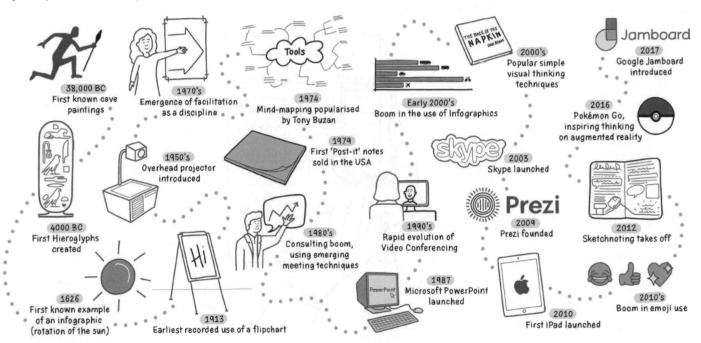

INFORMATION IS GOOD FOR YOU

It's official, information is good for you! The cave painters were inspired.

Meetings are absolutely bursting with data (by data I mean information in the broadest sense). Data before the meeting, usually in the form of pre-reads and the agenda. Data during the meeting, including slide decks and charts. Data following the meeting, typically the typed-up notes and shared decks. There is also all the digital data we receive on our smart phones and tablets, constantly reminding us that life goes on regardless of the meeting taking place.

And it's not just business and digital data we are bombarded with. Just think of all the less obvious but no less immediate information we process during the meeting, including non-verbal signals from our fellow meeting participants (such as the infamous raised eyebrow or knowing look), the physical environment we meet in, plus our own feelings and emotions. Frankly it's not surprising that we get tired quickly in meetings with all this data coming at us. No wonder we frequently dive for the biscuits and coffee to keep us going.

It is precisely because there is so much information available to us every minute that we, as meeting leaders, have a responsibility – or even a duty – to ensure that the information we use, including quantity, in our own meetings is selected well and used responsibly. But we're not simply doing this in the spirit of being 'nice'. The information we choose to use in our meetings must align to the meeting's purpose and help us achieve our desired outcomes. After all, if it does not fit with the purpose, then what's the point of using it? But more about that in Section 3 when I introduce you to the Meeting Kaleidoscope.

INFORMATION IS SOCIAL

Every meeting I run can be described as a highly visual *and* social occasion. Why? Because I have developed the habit of:

1. ensuring that the information to be shared in the meetings is carefully considered beforehand,
2. planning what form the information should take in order to serve the group to make the best possible decision, and
3. using the information flexibly during the meeting so that it serves the social interaction and thinking of the group, rather than the other way around.

Meetings are social occasions where information is shared, exchanged, analysed and processed with the aim of reaching not just any decision, but an excellent decision. I have yet to run a meeting that does not include an important aspect of data; it's virtually impossible to do!

If we follow this line of thought it stands to reason that information is a social tool, and it plays a transformative role in our 'meeting lives' (in which you will remember we supposedly spend about 50% of our time). In the preface of their updated book *The Social Life of Information*, Brown and Duguid introduce us to Vicesimus Knox, an English writer, headmaster and priest who, in 1778, declared that his was the 'age of information'. During that time which, like now, was marked by significant social and political change, the telegraph was emerging as a breakthrough method of communication, accompanied by the development of all things steam.

Rather like a teenager examining a fax machine we may laugh loudly at this 'age of information' in all its crude simplicity, but Knox was right, his was the age of information – but then, isn't every age?

> 'Knox closely connected popular democracy and information when he declared that if the people are given "fair and full information…they will do the thing that is right in consequence of it."…While the technologies have changed, that faith in the transformative power of information survives.'
>
> Brown and Duguid, 2017

Fast forward to today, when the term 'information' is strongly linked to technology and social media, and the whole integrity of information itself is making headline news with 'fake news' and 'post-truth' part of our everyday vocabulary.

UNDERSTANDING INFORMATION

In Section 1 we explored the definition of a meeting, but let's remind ourselves of what is meant by information.

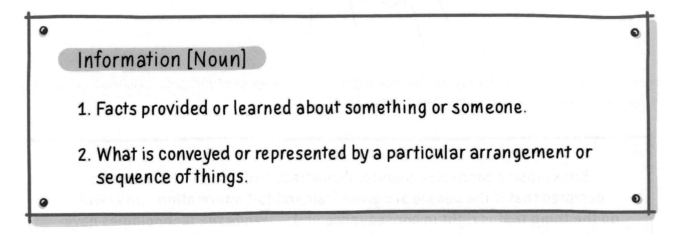

Information [Noun]

1. Facts provided or learned about something or someone.

2. What is conveyed or represented by a particular arrangement or sequence of things.

With meetings in mind, the most important words in this definition are (1) **learning** and (2) **sequence**. In our everyday meetings we bring and share information in the spirit of helping each other learn about the topic we are discussing and to make good decisions. To do that, we need to introduce the information in a sequence that allows us to build our knowledge to the point of being able to make the right decision.

This is great, everybody helping one another and all moving forward together, hooray! If this is your experience then I salute both you and your organisation – keep up the great work! On the other hand, your experience may be somewhat different. We all know the expression 'information is king' and whoever holds it has all the power. The meeting culture of an organisation, and how information is shared, can often be a window into the organisation's culture. I love the description 'fair and full information' used by Brown and Duguid, meaning that the people who use it have the opportunity to do the right thing.

How many times have you been in a situation when, had you the right information at the time, you would have made a completely different decision?

Let's summarise. Firstly, we know that information has the power to transform. We've seen that in the earlier timeline of visual language and the effect these tools have had on our lives, both personal and business. Secondly, we know that meetings are simply exchanges of data, although the data itself may not be so simple. Thirdly, how we share the information can have a critical impact on the success of our meetings.

MEETING CULTURE

There is a saying that 'the organisation takes on the personality of its CEO'. This is a super insight, and one I have personally witnessed, particularly during a transition of leadership where the outgoing people-focussed CEO was succeeded by a CEO very much preoccupied with data. Equally valid, but very different approaches.

It follows that the style of meetings in an organisation (the meeting culture) often takes the lead from the wider organisation's culture, including the various 'meeting mistakes' that become embedded in everyday practice. Below you will find a few characters you may recognise in your organisation, and the typical meeting information mistakes they make.

The Maverick ('Never knowingly prepared')

The Maverick races from one meeting to the next. They will arrive at the meeting room at the same time as their colleagues and will be busy setting up at the very time the meeting is due to start. It's not surprising that they use their slides so often given the ease with which a computer can be plugged in. The Maverick spends a large amount of their time dealing with logistical hurdles, such as when the projector doesn't link to the computer, or there aren't enough flipchart pages left, or the marker pens have gone missing. Most likely to say, 'I'll be with you in 2 minutes!'

The Bomber ('Data – dumped')

The Bomber's weapons of choice are large presentations, heavy reports and detailed figures sent to all participants to read and absorb. Typically, the Bomber will feel hugely relieved once the data is deployed on target. This could be because they have been instructed to send the pre-reads out to meeting participants by 'the boss'. Does the Bomber care whether colleagues will have the time to read, let alone absorb, the information? Most likely to say, 'Just a little pre-read.'

Captain Instant ('Let's meet now')

Captain Instant lives in a meeting universe where everything can be done immediately and, above all, according to their own diary. If there's a meeting to be had, it will take place when Captain Instant wants it to happen, regardless of whether others have the time. Maybe they are waiting to meet you now? Captain Instant's trademark is an electronic meeting invitation for a time that clashes with your other diary commitments. Most likely to say, 'I'm ready now, are you?'

The Blanket ('In the comfort zone')

The Blanket prefers to share their information in a format that is comfortable and appeals to them rather than considering the preferences and characteristics of those on the receiving end. Trusted, sage and reliable is their mantra. For example, this could be a slide deck presentation or detailed spreadsheets. The Blanket so enjoys sharing information in this way that they see no other method of reaching the same result. Most like to say, 'As you will see in row 264, column RR.'

The Hoarder ('Information retainer')

The Hoarder likes to keep firm hold of information. Sharing the knowledge might be useful for others but this data is precious! Not only is holding the information important, but letting others know they have it is a huge source of satisfaction. They may give a little away here and there, but only in carefully controlled doses. Most likely to say, 'Why do you need to know that?'

The Hammer ('Forcing content')

The Hammer's aim is to pack as much information into the allocated time as possible. If they are given 10 minutes to present (plus 5 minutes Q&A), they will stretch it to 25. The Hammer has little understanding that a 58-slide deck may not align with the 10 minutes they have available; however it's full steam ahead as they fail to notice the body language of participants or the hand signal to stop. Most likely to say, 'Just a couple more slides.'

Do you recognise any of these characters? Maybe you notice some of these behaviours and habits in your own approach to meetings. In which case it's time to grasp the meeting bull by the horns and make a change, today.

HOW CAN I MAKE A CHANGE?

In my work as a meeting leader I am often approached by individuals who wish their meeting culture to be disrupted, forced out of a rut, to become engaging, energising and productive. However, these wishes are often accompanied by a strongly held belief that things will never change because meetings are always conducted in a certain way.

Whilst it could be revolutionary, top management are unlikely to spend time focussing on changing an organisation's meeting culture, if for no other reason than there are plenty of more pressing matters to discuss in the current fast-changing world of business. Waiting for a signal from the top is likely to be a long one. The metaphorical oil tanker may take a very long time to turn.

My response is not to see this as a mammoth challenge, but as a superb opportunity to act as a role model for amazing meeting practice and to make brave choices about the way you choose to run your meetings. After all they are your meetings, aren't they?

It's time to be **BRAVE** with your information choices, as it's hugely tempting to fall into the groove of 'that's how it's done around here'. I urge bravery not for the thrill of it (although a thrilling meeting is a great thing) but in the spirit of your every meeting being hugely productive both for you and for your meeting participants.

Do you want to be BRAVE? Here's how. . .

Balanced:

Aim to provide information in a variety of formats. Large amounts of numerical data can be difficult to absorb, whereas pictorial information might be easier to process. By focussing on providing a range of data types you are more likely to convey your message successfully, especially in large groups and cross-functional meetings.

In your next meeting, use at least three different methods of visually communicating information, using the visual tools in Section 6 of this book. Be sure to find out what resources are available in your meeting space first, so you can be sure you can make it happen.

Relevant:

Ask yourself, is the information (or Content as I will describe in Section 3) being shared in your meeting relevant to the purpose of the meeting? If not, ditch it. Focus your meeting participants on what's important by being selective with the data you use – anything else may prove to be a distraction and take your meeting participants' focus away from the conversations you need to have.

Review the information you intend to share either before or in your next meeting. Aim to remove 50% of the information, leaving only the core content. For example, if you have 10 slides planned, reduce it to five and make the message punchy and concise.

Accessible:

How is your information being shared? Everyone knows that lengthy pre-reads don't always get read, but they continue to be sent. By filtering the information that is essential you will be doing yourself and your meeting participants an immense favour. If you need to send large amounts of information before or during the meeting, include an executive summary, or could the summary on its own be just perfect for generating enough understanding for the conversation to take place?

Create a summary, of no more than one page, of the data you are sending out to meeting participants. If absolutely necessary you can still send the 'heavy data' with it. In the meeting why not ask your participants for feedback on how useful they found the summary as a way of being prepared for the next meeting?

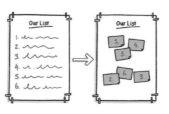

Versatile:

When you are planning your meeting, and the information you are sharing, consider whether these elements link together. For example, tasking the group to generate a list of ideas on a flipchart can be a super quick way of generating possibilities, but what happens if you want to cluster that data into themes in the next part of the process?

What you can do...

When planning your meeting, consider inputs and outputs. If the outputs from one part of the meeting are the inputs to the next, make sure that the data you have generated can be worked with easily for a smooth transition and ease of understanding.

Energising:

The information used in the meeting needs to capture interest and motivate people to interact with it. This will often depend on human elements such as learning styles. Is the way you have communicated your information visually interesting, such as making use of compelling imagery? How much opportunity do your meeting participants have to interact with the information provided?

What you can do...

Find two colleagues whom you know have a different style of working with information compared to you. Ask them to give you feedback on how you are planning to share the information in the meeting and incorporate their insights into your planning so that you maintain participants' interest.

THINK PARTICIPANT

If I were to offer you one BIG piece of advice in this section, it is to **think participant**. Of course this applies not simply to the information used in the meeting but to all aspects of running a meeting. Information is so very critical to the effectiveness of a meeting that it deserves special mention.

There are two reasons for this statement. Firstly, I use the term 'participant' very deliberately, because by its very nature there is implied involvement in the meeting. In many cases meeting participants are described in passive terms such as the 'audience', 'attendees' or 'delegates'. What's missing here is a belief that, in order to contribute to a successful meeting, people need to actively engage in the meeting itself. If you start with the mindset that the people in your meeting are participants, you are off to a powerful start.

Secondly, information is 'not a mallet'. As the Hammer will soon learn, it doesn't necessarily follow that meeting participants will understand your message any more deeply or clearly if you use a greater volume of information to force the message home. All information tools, including slide decks, can be extremely powerful if used well. It is the choices you make about **HOW** you use the information that will make a significant difference to the success of your meeting.

YOUR ORGANISATION'S MEETING CULTURE

How would you describe the meeting culture in your organisation? What do you notice when you compare various meetings taking place in your department, or with other teams? There are likely to be similarities in the way meetings are organised and conducted which give you a clue as to how meetings are regarded.

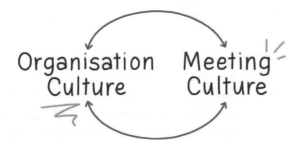

Reflect on the characteristics of meetings using the headings below, and mind-map your thoughts. From this you should be able to develop an understanding of the meeting culture in your organisation. If you're not sure how to mind-map, check out Tool 13 in Section 6.

How are meetings arranged?

MY ORGANISATION'S
MEETING CULTURE...

What behaviours do I notice
in the meetings I attend?

How do we manage information
before and during meetings?

In Section 3 I will introduce you to two approaches that will help you understand more deeply your role as a meeting leader, reinforce the importance of how you use information in your meetings and help you master sequence to great effect.

THE GOLDEN NUGGETS

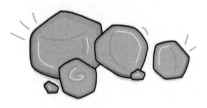

- Every one of us is wired to think visually to some degree.
- Working visually is powerful when working across cultures, including business functions.
- Spotting the characters who form barriers to good visual meeting practice will enable you to take positive action with the information you choose to use.
- Be BRAVE and choiceful when you select visual tools and information to work with.
- Treat your meeting participants as just that – participants.
- Your organisation's culture will impact upon the meeting culture. What can you can do to positively disrupt this loop?

Add your own golden nuggets, insights and inspiration here. . .

TIN KALEIDOSCOPES AND THE TYRANNY OF URGENCY – TWO MODELS TO HELP YOU ACE YOUR MEETINGS

In Section 2 I introduced you to the reasons why you should take a visual approach in your meetings, where this visual way of working has evolved from, your meeting culture and the characters you might meet along the way. In this section I will explain two approaches which will firstly help you refine your thinking as you prepare to lead your meetings, and secondly serve to make your meetings more productive and engaging with the support of powerful visual tools.

TIN KALEIDOSCOPES

When you were child you may have owned one of these – a tin kaleidoscope. Although less likely to make it to the Christmas toy top 10 now, the kaleidoscope is a fascinating toy that delivers completely different results every time it is played with.

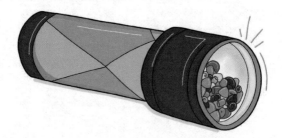

The term 'kaleidoscope' originated from the early 1800s and derives from the Ancient Greek 'kalos' – meaning beauty; 'eidos' – meaning that which is seen in form and shape; and 'skepeo' – meaning to look, examine and observe beautiful forms (source: Wikipedia). Although very simple in construction, the kaleidoscope is a wonderful visual tool, and probably one we learn to appreciate more as adults than as children.

With more years of experience running meetings than we can remember, my business partners and I wanted to find a simple visual way of conveying the key elements that should form the primary focus of any meeting leader. We had seen plenty of concepts and models on our travels but finding one that resonated with us was proving tricky, until we came across a simple tin kaleidoscope, and the rest is history.

The beauty of the kaleidoscope is that it only takes a very small turn to create a different visual image through the lens, and this is a perfect metaphor for your work as a meeting leader, where you are constantly making small changes and interventions which affect the meetings you lead.

For example, there will be times when you ask a very simple question in the meeting, invite a quiet participant into the conversation, or focus the group's attention on a particular chart or slide. Like the small turn of the kaleidoscope, every small 'move' you make as a meeting leader *will* have an impact upon your meeting, whether you make those 'moves' consciously or not.

It's time for me to introduce you to the Meeting Kaleidoscope, and how this simple tool can help you make effective choices with the visual information you choose to use in your meetings.

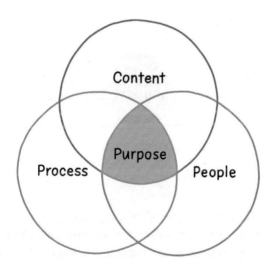

The Meeting Kaleidoscope is comprised of three core interdependent elements – **Content**, **Process** and **People**, held together by a central point – **Purpose**. You can discover much more about this model in *The Meeting Book* by my business partner Helen Chapman; however I will outline the tool here and add an emphasis on visual information.

PURPOSE

At the core of the Meeting Kaleidoscope is Purpose. This should always be the starting point for your meeting – every time.

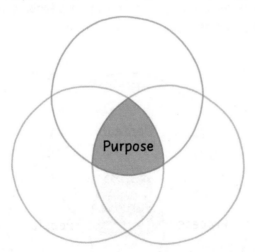

How many meetings have you attended where the purpose of the meeting is unclear, or completely unknown? It's astounding how many people tell me they accept meeting invitations from colleagues when they have absolutely no idea what the meeting is about or why they need to attend; nonetheless they go ahead and attend without seeking clarification as to why. This is ridiculous!

If you wish to avoid being the leader of one of these meetings, ask yourself this question right now. . .

'Is the purpose of the next meeting I am running fully aligned with my organisation's purpose?'

It doesn't matter at all what the purpose of your organisation is. It could be manufacturing hi-tech vacuum cleaners, growing trees, caring for animals, exploring Mars, finding the cure for cancer, or delivering cost-effective services through the internet. The point is that the purpose of your meeting must be in complete alignment with that of your organisation and, if it's not, then why are you bothering? There are millions of meetings taking place around the world each day that have no clear purpose and do not serve their organisation – please don't make your meeting one of those.

What's your organisation's purpose? You may know it intimately, but if not it's worthwhile checking and noting it down in the thought bubble below. By the way, if you don't know you won't be the first or last person not to. Simply by identifying it here could help you to communicate it to others who may be in the same position as you.

● MY ORGANISATION'S PURPOSE:

Check the agenda of your next meeting. From which items on your agenda can you draw a metaphorical 'straight line' to why your organisation exists? If there are items on the agenda that do not link to the organisation's purpose remove them and find another way of addressing those points. Maybe they could be dealt with by e-mail?

In the simple table below, list the items you are planning to discuss at your next key meeting, and consider whether they truly align with the purpose of both your organisation and your meeting. For those that you tick 'Not aligned', find another way to approach these points which saves you valuable time for the points that are aligned.

MY ORGANISATION'S PURPOSE IS ...		
MY MEETING'S PURPOSE IS ...		
MEETING ITEMS:	ALIGNED TO PURPOSE	NOT ALIGNED TO PURPOSE

If there's one thing you can do now that will start to differentiate your meetings from others it is clearly communicating the purpose to the people you invite in advance.

Do you remember the meeting scenarios mentioned earlier? Here are two contrasting e-mails inviting participants to the meeting. You will be able to guess which e-mail belongs to which meeting!

I guarantee you that your participants will feel more engaged and informed just by telling them why the meeting is important, and why they need to be there. Try it and see what happens.

Christmas Product Meeting

To: Management Team   Today at 15:04

Subject: Christmas Product Meeting

From: CEO Office

The CEO wants you to attend this meeting and bring an idea for our new Christmas product.

We will aim to start at 10am, and the meeting will be in the Board Room.

Thanks,

Secretary to the CEO

Christmas Product Meeting

To: Management Team   Today at 15:09

Subject: Christmas Product Meeting

From: CEO Office

Dear Management Team,

I am delighted to invite you to attend the Christmas Product Exploration meeting on Monday at 10am. The meeting will be held in the 'New Frontier' meeting room on the 1st floor where we will have plenty of space to work. The meeting will conclude at 1pm and lunch will be provided.

You have been invited to this meeting as a key function leader with deep knowledge of new product development and launch.

Meeting Purpose:
The purpose of the meeting is to explore and identify viable options for our new Christmas product, with the intention of scoping shortlisted ideas for testing.

Meeting Outcomes:
The outcomes of the meeting are:

- Alignment on the types of product that will win in the marketplace based on input from all key business functions
- An agreed shortlist of viable products for initial testing and prototyping
- Agreement on tangible next steps and timetable for delivery

Please read the latest industry trends summary (attached). There will be additional copies, plus further information available at the meeting for you all to access whilst we work together.

I would be grateful if you could confirm your attendance by tomorrow at 5pm and please do let me know if you have any specific dietary requirements.

Thank you,

Secretary to the CEO

CONTENT

Purpose draws together the three core components of the kaleidoscope. The first is Content.

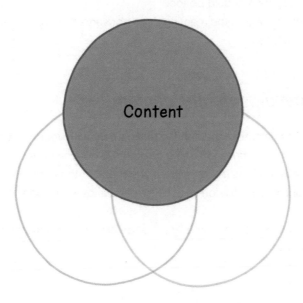

It is truly difficult to have a meeting without content. The content includes the data and information we explored previously. Strategy, business plans, performance figures, health and safety reports *and* spontaneous content that is offered by meeting participants in conversation.

Step 1: Does your content align with your meeting purpose?

Check that the content you are proposing to discuss aligns with and serves your meeting purpose. If your meeting purpose is aligned to your organisation's purpose then your content should be too.

If the content you are proposing to introduce into the meeting does not serve the purpose it will create an unnecessary distraction and will not be adding any value. Don't include it.

Step 2: How can I best communicate this content?

Ask what's the most effective way of communicating and sharing this content with your meeting participants, both before and during the meeting, so that it serves the people in your meeting to have productive conversations and make the best decisions.

The choices you make about the content will, like the 'moves' you make in the meeting itself, impact upon the success of your meeting. If you keep in mind that the content you use forms a 'twist' of your kaleidoscope, then you are starting in the right frame of mind.

Sadly, the consequence of not considering content carefully either before or during the meeting can be seen in Section 2, such as the prevalence of the Bomber or the Blanket.

PEOPLE

If you thought having a meeting without content was difficult, try having a meeting without People. Some say that meetings would be perfect if it wasn't for the people attending and, whilst this might appear to be true in some cases, the fact is that people tend to be incredibly useful in meetings!

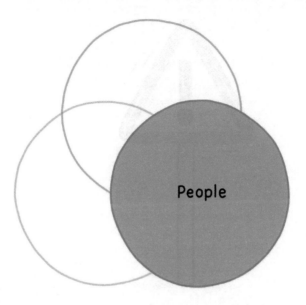

Just as you asked yourself whether the content of your meeting served your meeting's purpose, so you should test whether the people you have invited to your meeting are the right people to be there. We know from experience it is tempting to invite a range of people in the hope that most will be able to attend, or that some will bring knowledge of the content and will be able to contribute something of value. The reality is that many attend meetings without any understanding as to why they have been invited, and if it's not obvious to them, is it obvious to you?

Warning! It's easy to invite people to our meetings whom we consider to be similar to us. We've all done it, probably because we regard these people as having a similar perspective to us, or they are likely to be in agreement with what we are aiming to achieve. After all, how tempting is it to invite someone to your meeting who you know is likely to disagree with you or has an even better idea than yours?

Diversity and inclusion must play a key role in whom you invite to your meetings *but* I urge you to think well beyond the typical definitions of diversity such as gender, age and ethnicity, to a far broader and more versatile definition about diversity of thinking and perspective. Remember, everyone on this planet offers a different perspective – after all no one else can offer the same perspective as you.

In his book *The Medici Effect*, Frans Johansson explains how diversity of thinking can create a real advantage in the context of innovation. By explaining the distinction between directional ideas (generated by people operating within the same field/discipline) and intersectional ideas (generated by people from different fields/disciplines) he creates a powerful case for embracing difference rather than homogeneity.

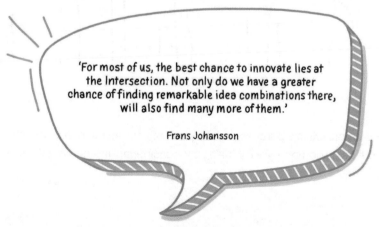

'For most of us, the best chance to innovate lies at the Intersection. Not only do we have a greater chance of finding remarkable idea combinations there, will also find many more of them.'

Frans Johansson

Although inviting people with very different perspectives might initially appear inconsistent with your meeting's purpose, in reality this approach demonstrates powerful thinking when compared to selecting on traditional diversity criteria alone. When planning your next meeting, consider which people might offer valuable and different perspectives.

Earlier you considered your organisation's purpose, the purpose of your meeting, and the meeting items you need to discuss that are aligned with the purpose. Now build upon your thinking by considering the perspectives you need for each conversation, and who is best to provide them.

MY ORGANISATION'S PURPOSE IS ...		
MY MEETING'S PURPOSE IS ...		
MEETING ITEMS	THE PERSPECTIVES I NEED ARE	WHO IS THE BEST PERSON TO PROVIDE IT

PEOPLE AND VISUAL INFORMATION

You've reflected on the group of people you wish to invite to your meeting. They demonstrate an impressive diversity of perspective which will add immense value to your content and align with your purpose.

When it comes to selecting visual information to assist this group ask yourself the following questions for each person, bearing in mind that a group is a collection of individuals, and they may have very different preferences.

Add in the name of the people you are planning to invite and what observations you have of them, using the guide questions below. If you don't know, just ask.

- What do I know about this group's thinking and working style?
- What types of information do they positively respond to?
- What types of information turn them off?

Reflecting on these questions will help you choose the most effective visual information methods for your meeting, and in Section 6 I will indicate how each tool might impact upon the core element of People.

PROCESS

The third element of the Meeting Kaleidoscope is Process. The first point to make clear is that this is *not* the agenda, which is a list of topics to be discussed in a meeting in a specific order within the time available.

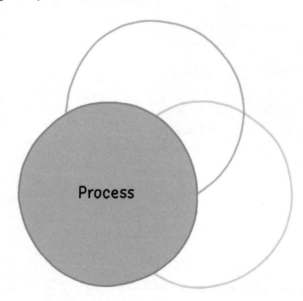

Process goes much deeper than the agenda by focussing on **HOW** the people in your meeting are going to work with the content at each point in your agenda. Whereas a conventional agenda is often seen as a series of independent points, your process design should incorporate all the items in one overall flow, with each item aligning and building on the other. Process could, in summary, be described as the HOW for your agenda.

It should be obvious that giving time to consider the purpose, content and people before you hold your meeting is critical. It is even more so for the process you design for your meeting, and subsequently the visual tools you intend to use to support the process. The challenge for many people in business is that time to prepare for meetings can be limited. My response is that more productive meetings will get significantly more done – who doesn't want that?

By this point you will have identified the agenda items for your meeting which align with your meeting's purpose, and you know whom you will be inviting to the meeting. The next stage is to consider the points on your agenda, and clarify **WHAT** you are aiming to achieve with each. A simple way of considering each point is to position it on this five-step model developed by Peter Senge. I often share this model, known as the Collaboration Continuum, when designing meetings as it helps to clarify what is expected of the people in the meeting. Each step in this diagram indicates the degree of influence or decision making the group has over the outcome of an agenda point.

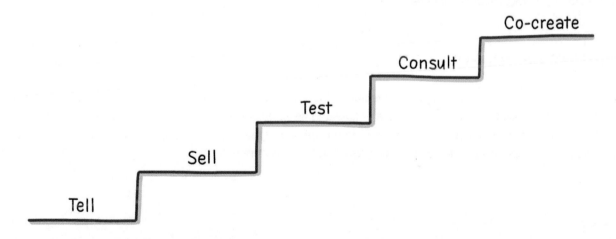

At which point on these steps do your meeting points sit? It is important to get this right as your group will be far more engaged if you are clear on what you are expecting of them and the degree of influence they have on a given topic. 'Sham consultation' is a common meeting error whereby participants are given the impression that they have influence over the outcome when in fact the decision has already been made.

Your choice of visual tools should complement what you are aiming to achieve at each point in your meeting, in support of your meeting purpose. For example, tools such as slide decks are useful in support of a 'tell' session (if you are conveying information about subjects or decisions that are unchangeable), whereas grids are useful for testing (comparing ideas against key criteria such as cost and effort), and drawings are powerful for co-creation (where the important details are determined by the group).

In Section 6 I will describe how each visual tool can support your process. I will also suggest where each tool may be most helpful on the five-step diagram.

The Meeting Kaleidoscope perfectly illustrates your dynamic role as a meeting leader. The meeting is a constantly changing form, and your small 'moves' and turns should utilise the content, make the best of the meeting participants, power up the process and nail your meeting outcomes.

It's time to introduce you to a second approach that I have found immensely useful as a meeting leader, and one that helps me to consider and select visual tools with confidence.

THE TYRANNY OF URGENCY

It's a fact that in any busy organisation time is hugely precious, and 'stuff' just needs to get done. As a result we have been conditioned to believe that long and detailed meetings are a waste of time and we should 'just get on with it and make a decision now'. I uphold this sentiment, but only in circumstances where just getting on with it and making a decision quickly is the right thing do to, and in many cases this approach serves poor decision making and a lack of commitment.

In this section I would like to introduce you to the work of Sam Kaner, which has underpinned much of my work in leading meetings.

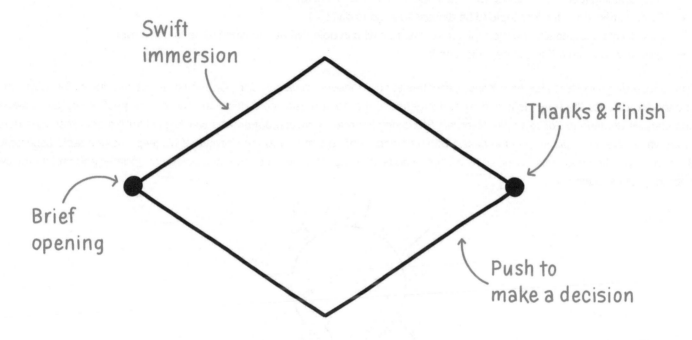

Swift immersion

Thanks & finish

Brief opening

Push to make a decision

Source: The Facilitator's Guide to Participatory Decision Making
- Sam Kaner

Many meetings in business work like this. . .

- Brief opening (perhaps referring to the last meeting and who's here)
- Swift immersion in the key topic to be discussed (time to diverge)
- Push to make a decision on the topic, agreement on who is doing what and when (time to converge)
- Thanks and finish (off to the next meeting?)

The above diagram illustrates how Kaner describes such a meeting in visual form. On the left is the starting point, with a brief divergence to discuss the topic, followed by convergence to the point of making a decision. And this is great, especially when the circumstances demand it. For example, General ('Storming') Norman Schwarzkopf Jr. was well known for his brief meetings during the Iraq war where he would stop in the desert with his troops, unfold a map upon the bonnet of his jeep, make a rapid assessment of the current position and make a decision on what to do next. Perfect for that scenario, or quick team updates and project reviews, but not for every situation.

Think of a meeting in which you have participated where a specific topic was discussed in detail for a long time. How did it feel for you? Slow, laborious, difficult? According to Kaner you were probably in the 'groan zone'. This is the point in a meeting where the group, supported by a meeting leader, focusses on a specific topic for an extended period, which can be frustrating and like 'walking in treacle'. Whilst being in this zone for the participants might appear difficult, Kaner has shown that by keeping participants in the 'groan zone' they are more likely to reach outcomes that they would never have encountered had they converged on the topic earlier and make robust decisions with more commitment.

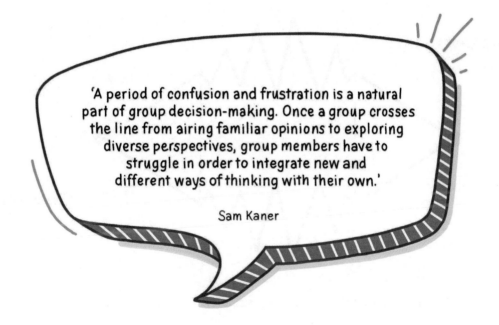

'A period of confusion and frustration is a natural part of group decision-making. Once a group crosses the line from airing familiar opinions to exploring diverse perspectives, group members have to struggle in order to integrate new and different ways of thinking with their own.'

Sam Kaner

Below I have illustrated how Kaner describes the flow of a meeting, including the 'groan zone'. In contrast to the previous diagram you will notice the 'spiked' middle section, which holds the group on the topic before converging on a decision. Leading the group at this point can be a challenge for any meeting leader, and if this is something that interests you I urge you to find out more as this could unlock some great outcomes for you and your group.

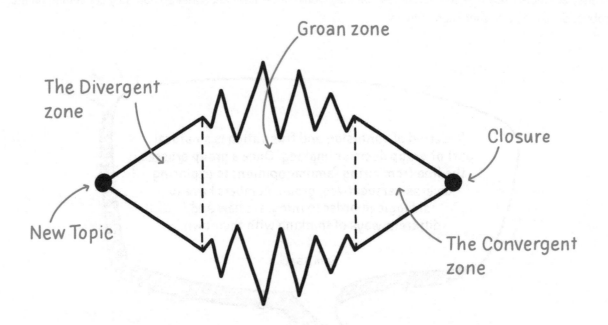

Source: The Facilitators Guide to Participatory Decision Making
- Sam Kaner

THE FIVE STAGES OF A SUCCESSFUL MEETING

OPENING   WORKING   STRETCHING   DECIDING   MOVING

At The Facilitation Partnership, as we share our thinking on successful meetings with our clients, we have taken inspiration from and built upon this approach to introduce five stages of a successful meeting.

1. *Opening:* Where the meeting starts. Focussing the participants on the meeting's purpose and desired outcomes, and creating a sense of community and building trust. Everyone is ready to get started on the work to be done.
2. *Working:* Where the action happens. Getting stuck into the content using the intended process for the meeting. By exploring the topic together the group shares perspectives, ideas and insights.
3. *Stretching:* Where the 'sticky bit' lies. Resisting the urge to converge and keeping the conversation focussed on the question at hand. Viewing the topic from a different perspective, testing and re-testing assumptions to reach a deeper understanding.

4. **Deciding:** Where converging commences. Based on the exploration during the Working and Stretching stages, the group decides on what decisions to make.
5. **Moving:** Where the momentum builds. The decisions have been made after much careful and detailed dialogue. This is the point where the group focusses on turning the decisions into action. Who will do what, when and how?

Source: The Facilitation Partnership Limited

For each of these stages there are decisions you need to make as a meeting leader about the visual tools you might use to support each stage, taking into consideration the content to be discussed, the people in the room, and your adopted process. Here are five examples to help you start your thinking:

Opening	PREP (Tool 2)
Working	Process Map (Tool 15)
Stretching	Push and Pull (Tool 22)
Deciding	Visual Voting (Tool 30)
Moving	Actions and Next Steps (Tool 35)

Do you recognise the above stages in your own meetings? Clearly there will be stages that you might recognise more than others, and indeed most stages, including the Opening, Working, Deciding and Moving, are generally to be found in all meetings, or at least they should be if the meetings are to be productive and successful in achieving their desired outcomes.

In Section 6 I will outline the various visual tools you can use in your meetings. I will also suggest which tools might be useful for the different stages of a successful meeting.

In the next section we will venture into another meeting world which has become increasingly common in our everyday lives – virtual meetings.

THE GOLDEN NUGGETS

- We frequently make small changes to how we run our meetings, all of which will have an impact on the group.
- The Meeting Kaleidoscope and the five stages of a successful meeting will act as your guide when planning and designing your meetings.
- Resist the urge to accept meeting invitations when you don't know the meeting purpose and why your presence is needed.
- Your meeting purpose *must* align with your organisation's purpose.
- The content you choose to discuss, the people you invite to the meeting, and the process you choose to adopt must align with your meeting's purpose.
- Leading your participants into the 'groan zone', where appropriate, will lead to richer conversation and commitment to decisions that stick.

Add your own golden nuggets, insights and inspiration here. . .

VIRTUAL, VISUAL AND VIRTUOUS – MAKING AN IMPACT EVEN WHEN THERE'S NO MEETING ROOM

THE LEGACY OF EYJAFJALLAJÖKULL

Do you remember where you were between 14 and 20 April 2010?

Maybe the name Eyjafjallajökull will jog your memory? Many people remember this period, mainly due to the travel chaos that ensued across Europe. Still no idea?

Eyjafjallajökull is the name of an island mountain glacier covering a volcano in southern Iceland. On 26 February 2010 seismic activity was recorded around the volcano, and in March 3,000 earthquakes were detected at its epi-centre. By mid-April the volcano was spewing out volcanic ash into the atmosphere across Europe. Twenty countries closed their airspace and approximately 10 million travellers had their travel plans changed or cancelled. The International Air Transport Association (IATA) estimated that the airline industry lost €148 million a day during the disruption (source: Wikipedia).

Departures

Flight	Destination	Status
AA6577	Frankfurt	Cancelled
EW8460	Berlin	Cancelled
BA853	Prague	Cancelled
9W8083	Atlanta	Cancelled
IB7412	Baltimore	Cancelled
BA7052	Madrid	Cancelled
ER8319	Belfast	Cancelled
GF6616	New York	Cancelled
KL1007	Amsterdam	Cancelled
AA6587	Nice	Cancelled

It seems likely we will never know the financial cost to business of this natural event, although I'd guess it was seismic (sorry, couldn't resist). I recall talk at the time quickly turning to the impact of this unforeseen event on meetings across the globe, and how businesses could continue to work effectively in the future even if people could not meet face to face. The answer – more virtual meetings!

Research and advisory firm Gartner were quick to publish their 'Out of the Ashes' report on the impact of Iceland's volcano, especially in terms of business continuity management.

'In the future, some organizations will look back in hindsight and say, "If only I'd mandated the use of video, I wouldn't have x of my staff strewn across the globe because aircraft have been grounded..."

Web conferencing, virtual worlds and remote collaboration vendors are experiencing unprecedented demand and will understandably prioritize existing customers...

These solutions are immediately available for download, scale well and provide workable solutions to an otherwise challenging problem.'

'Out of the Ashes'. Gartner. 2010

This isn't to assume that virtual meetings weren't commonplace before Eyjafjallajökull erupted; however they appeared to be a more widely considered option at this time. In our own business we quickly determined that virtual meetings would witness a huge surge and we should prepare for virtual 'lift-off' immediately – but after all the chaos in April 2010 it simply didn't happen to the extent we imagined. Rather than a volcanic rush, it was more of a puff of smoke.

Why did this happen? We spoke to many of our clients after the 'Icelandic Ash Cloud' and many told us they believed virtual meetings would increase in regularity; however they also said there is simply no substitute for an authentic face-to-face meeting.

Volcano or no volcano, it should be noted here that there is a general trend towards more flexible methods of working, supported by advances in technology, thus allowing people to work at home, or indeed anywhere they wish.

Various statistics and surveys point to an uplift in virtual working, although other measures indicate differences in opinion when it comes to the benefits of working virtually.

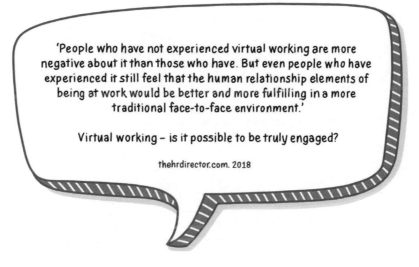

'People who have not experienced virtual working are more negative about it than those who have. But even people who have experienced it still feel that the human relationship elements of being at work would be better and more fulfilling in a more traditional face-to-face environment.'

Virtual working – is it possible to be truly engaged?

thehrdirector.com. 2018

VIRTUAL MEETINGS – THE GOOD, THE BAD AND THE UGLY

Without sounding like my father, there is no doubt that the ability to talk to someone on the other side of the world *and* see them at the same time is impressive. We've certainly come a long way since Vicesimus Knox's 'age of information'. Virtual meeting technology allows us to interact with the people we need and want to speak to, whether loved ones or business colleagues, in a way that the conventional telephone cannot offer.

There are, however, considerations to using this type of technology in the context of meetings. These are worth exploring before diving in to the world of virtual meetings particularly with regards to the use of visual information. So here we are – introducing the good, the bad and the ugly of virtual meetings.

The good...

Visible

You can see the person/people you are meeting with (video).

Fast

It's easy to talk to someone instantly.

Cost-effective

There's no need to book travel or a meeting venue.

Insightful

Participants are able to observe each other's non-verbal behaviour (e.g., body language).

Time-rich

Eliminated travel time makes for more time to be productive.

Portable

Virtual meeting technology can often be used in a variety of settings, such as with a mobile device.

Inclusive

The technology allows participants (small and large groups) from different geographies to contribute.

Data-friendly

Depending upon the platform used, visual information can be shared and updated during the meeting.

Safe

Technology may be beneficial for those who find face-to-face situations difficult.

The bad...

Glitchy

Technology can be problematic and affect conversation flow.

Noisy

Interference from the environments in which participants join the meeting can cause a distraction (e.g., car, busy public space).

Hidden

Even if the meeting involves a visible image of participants, such as a group, it can be difficult to see non-verbal behaviour.

Prohibitive

Quieter participants may be less likely to offer their contributions when others are speaking up.

Crossed

Talking over each other is common, especially where there is no facilitator to lead the conversation.

Loud

Share of voice can be easily dominated by the loudest participants, leaving others little or no chance to contribute.

Confused

Without the additional cues of non-verbal behaviour it can be difficult to understand others if one is not used to a particular language.

The ugly. . .

Distracting

Participating in a virtual meeting whilst doing other tasks, or even travelling, will result in reduced focus and attention (and can be dangerous!).

Sloppy

Participants may be inclined to allow their standards to slip, including punctuality.

Rude

'What the other person doesn't know won't hurt them.' It's not uncommon for people to behave in a way that they would never consider if they were in the room with others (e.g., eye-rolling, gestures).

Eyes up!

Everyone on the call is looking upwards towards a camera mounted on top of the TV screen. If you don't think this is off-putting, imagine your colleagues looking above your head every time they speak to you.

If you are new to the world of virtual meetings, and to some of the characteristics outlined above, I urge you to take a look at 'A Conference Call in Real Life' by Tripp and Tyler which can be found online. This is a wonderful four-minute film vignette of the types of problems experienced in virtual meetings. It will make you laugh and, if you have experience of virtual meetings, you may see behaviours that appear very familiar!

Before reading on, take a few minutes to consider the virtual meetings you have led or experienced. What worked well in those meetings, which would you like to see again in future, and if you could change your experience what might work better next time?

WHAT CURRENTLY WORKS WELL IN MY VIRTUAL MEETINGS?

WHAT WOULD IT TAKE TO MAKE THEM MORE EFFECTIVE?

What do you notice about your insights, and how could you use visual information more effectively in your virtual meetings to respond to these challenges?

Here are just a few of the comments we hear from leaders and participants of virtual meetings. . .

In Section 1 I explained that the purpose of this book is to explore how your meetings can be more engaging and productive through the effective use of visual information. This applies to virtual meetings too, but many challenges with virtual meetings cannot be resolved through the effective use of visual information alone.

Virtual meetings can be complex to lead, and whilst many are tempted to facilitate their own virtual meetings my recommendation is for all virtual meetings to be facilitated by someone who will lead the participants through the meeting process without becoming immersed in the content. This will allow participants to give their attention to the important topics being explored, whilst the facilitator ensures that everyone has a voice and the meeting achieves the desired outcomes.

AGREEING WAYS OF WORKING

If you are unable to secure a facilitator for your virtual meeting, ensure you spend time at the beginning of the meeting discussing and then explicitly agreeing on 'ways of working' so that all participants understand what is expected of each other in order to make the meeting a success. Others may know these as 'ground rules' or 'rules of engagement'. The purpose is not to be prescriptive and rule-bound, but to build trust and shine a light on good practice in service of achieving the meeting purpose together.

You might be leading a virtual meeting for the first time with a group of participants with whom you meet regularly on a face-to-face basis. This group may also have an established way of working that works well for them. As we know, virtual meetings are very different from face-to-face meetings, and so it is worthwhile being completely open and intentional about that difference.

CAPTURING WAYS OF WORKING

One doesn't need cutting-edge technology to create a list of ways of working in a virtual meeting. There are various ways this can be done even if you are not using a video conference. For example, you could. . .

- Capture them on a flipchart (if in a meeting room) and take a photo to send to all participants.
- Make a list on an e-mail and send to all.
- If you have it, use the facility on your web conference platform to capture the ways of working as text points, so everyone can see them.
- Ask participants to note them down as they are agreed.

GETTING VISUAL WITH THE VIRTUAL

When it comes to the use of visual information in virtual meetings there are a variety of approaches you can take that will focus participants on the purpose of the meeting and deliver on your desired outcomes.

Remember the Meeting Kaleidoscope – the content you choose to use for your virtual meetings must align with the purpose of your meeting, integrate with your chosen process, and be relevant to your meeting participants.

In Section 6 you will find a range of tools you can use in your meetings. I have indicated where I believe a tool could be used in a virtual meeting environment in the table of tools.

When compared to a meeting room a key challenge with virtual meetings is that the information you share cannot be placed around the room for participants to absorb and reflect on as the conversation progresses. The reality of virtual meetings often means that participants may be dialling in from hotels, airports or from home, in addition to meeting rooms in other offices.

Virtual meeting platforms are available that allow visual information to be created on the platform itself, or to be shared on the screen so everyone can view it at the same time. I urge you to explore the visual information capability of the platform you use or, if you have not chosen a platform to use yet, explore what is possible before making a decision.

10 TIPS TO BE MORE EFFECTIVE – VIRTUALLY

Below I have outlined 10 visual information tips to use when leading virtual meetings. I encourage you to consider these and cross-reference with the tool descriptions in Section 6.

The eagle eyed might be thinking that these could be used in many meetings, whether virtual or face to face, and they would be right, many of them are equally relevant. My desire to group them here is to simply emphasise that virtual meetings are often more challenging to lead as a facilitator, and so if you incorporate these practices into your meetings you are off to a powerful start.

Tip 1 – Share information beforehand

Preparation for virtual meetings can be even more critical for face-to-face meetings. Ideally pre-reads should be sent ahead of the meeting, with the meeting purpose and agenda, with clear guidance on what you expect participants to achieve before the meeting. Whilst it may be tempting not to share your slide deck etc., sharing it beforehand will help participants to absorb the information in advance so they come ready to ask questions in the call. You can still present on the call, but time will be given to generating meaning.

Tip 2 – Share your agenda

However you choose to present your agenda a big initial win is to ensure that everyone has a copy of the agenda (and the meeting purpose) before the meeting. If you are using a visual platform share the agenda visually at the outset of the meeting so everyone can see it. Talk it through briefly, explaining the flow and how the agenda supports the meeting purpose and, if you wish, the organisation's overall purpose. The more you can reinforce this latter point the more focussed your meeting participants are likely to be on the end goal.

Tip 3 – . . .and repeat

The start of the meeting is not the only time you should refer to your agenda. Revisit the agenda briefly as you progress through the meeting, orientating participants to the next step so they know what's next.

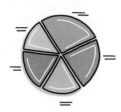

Tip 4 – Keep it simple

Virtual meetings can be a disorientating experience for many participants for the reasons given in the good, bad and the ugly. If the information you share is simply presented it will help your participants to maintain as much clarity of thought as possible. This is especially true for slide decks and reports. Remember to consider the people (as a group and individuals) in your virtual meeting and what type of information they might work with best.

Tip 5 – You are here

One of the most helpful things you can do for participants is to clearly direct them to what they need to read or view. You will have got off to a great start by orientating participants on the meeting agenda, and you can continue this by clearly explaining where they need to focus throughout the course of the meeting. If you are sharing slides, point out the area of the slide you are referring to.

Tip 6 – Flipcharts and photos

Just because your meeting is virtual doesn't mean that you can't use traditional methods to capture content. If you have a flipchart in your meeting room why not ask a participant to add points to the chart during your conversation (it helps if this is not you if you are leading the meeting, and you will need to make sure the participant taking notes isn't excluded from the conversation).

For virtual meetings on video your participants may be able to see the content as it emerges, or else you can summarise the contributions on the chart at key points or share a photo of the chart either by uploading it to the platform you are using or by sending to all via a mobile device. Remember that the content captured should reflect all contributions. If technology prevents you from understanding a specific point ask for clarity to ensure that no participant's contribution is excluded.

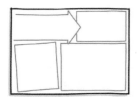

Tip 7 – Use templates that groups complete in the meeting

You might consider using printed visual templates that participants can populate during the meeting, especially if you have groups participating from different locations. A space for focussed group work in a virtual meeting can be a powerful method of engaging all participants in the conversation.

Tip 8 – Maintain an appropriate pace

Whilst not a visual tool per se, maintaining a pace that is helpful for all participants to keep up and have the opportunity to ask questions is vital in any virtual meeting. In audio-only virtual meetings it is common for meeting leaders to push ahead at speed given the absence of visual information (i.e., seeing the meeting participants) and therefore not notice that participants are struggling to keep up. Conversely it is common for participants finding it difficult to follow the pace to simply give up and disengage from the conversation altogether.

Tip 9 – A virtual visual buddy

If you are leading the meeting it's likely that you'll be fully absorbed in the conversation and ensuring that everyone is contributing. Why not ask someone in your meeting to take responsibility for visual information? This could be as simple as moving on the slide deck to setting up voting tools.

Tip 10 – Post-meeting communication

Sharing the visual information generated by the group right after the meeting is a sure way to keep momentum going and aid the implementation of agreed actions. Don't delay – send today!

IT'S OK TO BREAK AWAY

When we explored 'Process' within the Meeting Kaleidoscope we emphasised the importance of being clear about how the group will work on each point of your agenda. If you are leading your meeting face to face in a meeting room this might be easier as you have everything you need right there in the room, including resources, charts and the participants themselves.

A common misconception with virtual meetings is that the conversation needs to happen in one overall burst. By that I mean that participants remain on the call for a set period from start to finish. Just as you might design a process for participants to break into smaller groups when in a meeting room, you can do the same for virtual meetings, particularly where you have small groups of participants calling in from different locations.

We know that remaining on a long virtual meeting can be tiring and quickly reduces participant attention and energy especially where information, or the topic, is complex. The next time you need to plan an important virtual meeting, consider how you can design your process so that it enables participants to contribute in a way that allows them time away from the call itself.

In Section 5 we will explore how you can go about choosing the best visual tools for your meeting, whether virtual or face to face.

THE GOLDEN NUGGETS

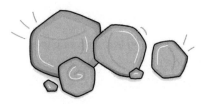

- The skills needed to lead a virtual meeting are different from the skills needed to lead a face-to-face meeting.
- Agreeing ways of working at the outset will focus participants on how to make the virtual meeting a success.
- There are many different ways visual information can be captured in a virtual meeting, both electronically and using traditional pen and paper.
- Keep information simple and orientate participants throughout the meeting.
- Ask someone to 'buddy' you as meeting leader by taking responsibility for the visual information shared in the meeting.
- Participants don't have to be online from start to finish. Break-out sessions can work virtually too.

Add your own golden nuggets, insights and inspiration here. . .

NERDY NIBS AND CIRCULAR NIGHTMARES – GET TOOLED UP AND PLAN FOR SUCCESS

Here we are. You are about to become acquainted with the visual tools you will use to lead meetings with impact. Before you get started I have practical advice to offer you on how you might go about selecting and creating your visual tools, including the resources that will make this easier. I strongly recommend you read this section before delving into the tools.

The 'devil is in the detail', and in our experience the success of any meeting is, in large part, a result of the preparation that is put into it. If we adopt the positive framing we explored in Section 1 the time we dedicate to planning and designing meetings will reap rewards in productivity and engagement. It's a fact.

YOU, THE VISUAL MEETING DESIGNER

You (yes, you) can design your own visual resources to make your meetings more impactful, productive and engaging. Many of the tools in Section 6 can be created easily on a flipchart or large sheet of paper. You will need to tailor these tools to your own meeting needs, and that is simple too. Read on to explore the recommended kit to help you do just that.

> Remember, a well-designed, impactful chart does NOT equal a successful meeting.
> Your meeting purpose, planning and design must come first, and your charts will naturally follow on from your planning.

WHAT'S IN YOUR TOOLKIT?

The well-prepared meeting leader will always have the right resources to hand in order to design and lead an impactful meeting, and this doesn't mean a budget-busting spending spree at the local office supplies store. What do you have in your meeting kitbag right now?

Below I have listed items that I think you will need to have, and those that might be a nice-to-have. Focus on the need-to-haves now, and you will have enough to start your preparation.

Paper roll or flipchart

I love working BIG, using a large roll of paper to maximise both participant working space and possibilities. Paper rolls, in white or brown, are widely available. Working with the humble meeting room flipchart is just as versatile, especially in meetings with smaller groups or constrained spaces. Remember, you can still work big by fixing a number of flipchart sheets to the wall together. By the way, don't forget to keep a sharp edge knife to cut your paper if you are using large paper rolls.

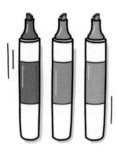

Marker pens

Good quality markers are the meeting leader's best friends. Check your pens regularly to ensure they are juicy and ready for their next excursion. I always prefer to work with a core set of pens, including 'cool' colours such as dark blue and brown, plus a couple of 'hot' colours such as orange and red. Black is also a must.

Yellow is often difficult for participants to see, so I tend not to provide yellow pens for participants to use. Pale yellow can be helpful to you, as you can write points on your chart as prompts to you, which are less visible.

Of course, you can choose whichever colours you wish, but remember that water-based markers are less likely to bleed through the paper, which means that leaving your writing on the wall, literally, is much less likely to happen.

If you can obtain refillable marker pens, that will also save you money in the long term and will prove to be a more environmentally sustainable option.

Finally, keeping a range of markers with thick and thin nibs will also prove useful. Thicker pens tend to be great for headings, but not so good for detailed content.

Here's a tip. Try fixing a strip of tape around your core set of pens so they are fixed together in a row. No more hunting for the pen you put down, as all your core pens are safely connected and can be easily held when you are in action.

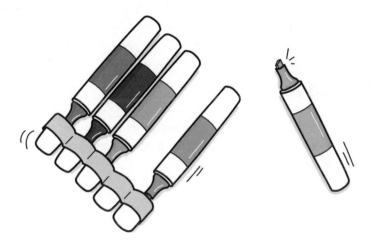

Sticky notes

Always highly useful and versatile. Rather than buying small sticky notes try larger sizes (e.g., A5) so participants can write on them with plenty of space available. Using sticky notes in a variety of colours can be a useful way of distinguishing content if necessary, or if not it simply makes the output more visually interesting.

Tape

Good quality tape is a must. Sticky alternatives for fixing paper to the wall are often great for small items but can be prone to damaging walls and tearing your charts. Good quality artists or masking tape won't cost the earth, and definitely less than the cost of repainting the meeting room wall.

White address labels

We all make mistakes, and white address labels are a super quick way of covering up an error so you can move on with confidence, especially when designing your charts ready for the meeting. Keep a roll of these in your kitbag just in case.

Camera

Everyone carries a camera now, right? Have yours to hand, especially when the meeting finishes, and you can take pictures of all the outputs and send these to your meeting participants in double quick time. No more waiting for meeting minutes to be typed up and distributed.

Long ruler or straight edge

A real advantage for taking the wiggle out of your straight lines. Also good for measuring out space on charts such as grids and tables.

THE NICE-TO-HAVES

Sticky voting dots

There will be times when your meeting participants need to express their preference for an idea or concept through a vote. Keeping a stock of sticky dots can aid this process, although if you have marker pens to hand you can ask participants to clearly mark their preference.

Large compass

If drawing circles gives you sleepless nights a large compass is the antidote. Beware of compasses with sharp points as they can rip your chart.

Soft pastels

Soft chalk pastels can add eye-catching depth and colour to your charts. Adding a tint around a border will draw the eye into the content. Apply with a tissue to create different depths of tone.

GET TO KNOW YOUR PEN FRIEND

Nib facts

I always use chisel tip markers because they give me so much more flexibility with the line I draw when compared to a bullet tip. Did you know there are three types of lines you can generate from one chisel tip marker?

The broadside	the widest part of the nib, allowing you to draw the thickest lines. These can be great for underlining a title or drawing a line border around your charts.
The tip	right at the top of the nib, the tip gives you freedom to write clearly without being too thick or too thin.
The heel	a small part of the nib at the bottom of the broadside. You can draw fine lines with the heel, but it will take some practice!

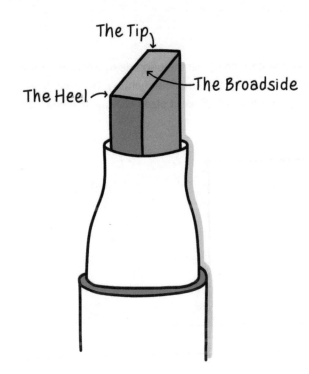

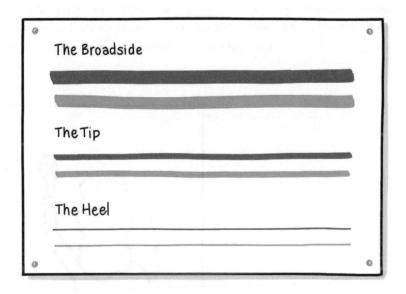

Drawing straight lines

The best way of perfecting your skills on the pens is to practise, practise and practise some more. To start, try drawing a range of horizontal lines on a flipchart or sheet of paper using the broadside, tip and heel. If you try marker pens of different sizes too you can create lines of many different thicknesses.

Drawing circles

Drawing perfect circles is certainly not a skillset of mine; however if I practise without letting the nib hit the paper first, then I am more likely to draw a near perfect circle than if I just go for it. This takes advantage of something called muscle memory, because tasks using one's muscles often appear to be easier after practising. Now try drawing some circles of different sizes using whichever part of the nib you prefer.

USE OF COLOUR

We all have our favourite colours, although it's good to know that not all colours are suitable when leading a meeting. My favourite colour is yellow, which is generally useless for meetings (as mentioned above). Below I have listed a range of colours I tend to use when leading meetings. You can certainly choose your own colours; however my guidance is to be consistent in how you use your colours as you design your charts and lead your meeting.

Black – my first choice, always easy to read and does the job.

Brown – a 'cool' colour which offers something different from black.

Blue – a smart cool colour similar to brown, always a reliable member of the team.

Green (dark) – a positive can-do colour, good for conversations about growth and getting things done.

Red – the hottest of all colours, great for underlining and bullets, with warning connotations. A bit shouty if used to write text.

Orange – red's best friend, a warm tone for highlighting.

Grey – cool and calm, great for adding shadows to fonts.

Yellow – happy and cheerful, although difficult for participants to read.

A tip to use when creating lists is to use alternate colours for each point on the list. For example, a combination of two cool colours, such as black, blue or green, used alternately will help your meeting participants to see where one point on the list ends and another one starts.

SIMPLE FONTS

A valuable piece of advice I can offer when preparing your charts is not to regard them as artistic masterpieces. The most important characteristic, and the measure of success, of your charts will be the extent to which they serve the group in generating meaning and achieving the meeting purpose, which of course will be aligned with the organisation's purpose. In fact, I will be so bold as to say that whatever you create your group will love.

Below you will find a range of font styles, most of which you can use for titles and headings when designing your charts. When you are working in the moment, select a style that is both legible to the group and comfortable for you to work with at pace. These are also created using different parts of the nib, described above. Read on and see tip 2 about using lower-case text when writing at speed.

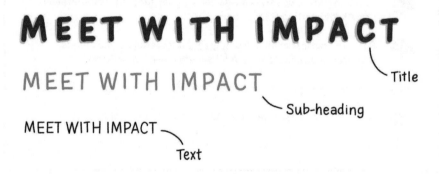

DRAWING BULLETS

Bullets are a super simple way of drawing attention to a piece of text. There are so many different bullets one can choose, and here are just a few that you might want to try. A tip to remember is to use a colour that contrasts with your text. For example, using red or orange bullets stands out well when using cool colours for your text, such as black, green and blue.

SIMPLE SHAPES

Although many charts will contain valuable content in the form of text, there are a range of simple shapes you can use when creating your charts. Many of these are related to human interaction, thinking and exploring. Some may be shapes in which you can insert headings to give your charts more impact.

Here are a small range of simple shapes that you may find useful when designing your charts. Try practising them on a flipchart using a marker pen.

You don't need to be an artist to create a range of simple and engaging icons, as many are a combination of simple shapes. Many of the tools in Section 6 feature simple icons you can use on your own charts, and as you continue working visually you will soon build your own visual vocabulary, including icons that are more relevant to your own organisation.

WRITING TEXT IN THE MOMENT

The world of a meeting leader is a complex one. There's so much to be attuned to, such as the behaviour of the group, the information being discussed, and whether the process you have designed is working. Not only are you thinking about what's happening right now, but your mind is also focussed on the next stage of the meeting and how to transition successfully.

'Don't do yourself what you can get the group to do for you.'

The saying above is a valuable one to remember, especially when it comes to capturing visual information. Let's imagine you are leading a meeting where the group need to offer ideas, which will be captured on a list. Will you be the person capturing the content or will you ask someone in the group to do it for you? There's no right or wrong answer. If you choose to do it yourself you will have control over what's being captured, whereas if you ask a member of the group to do it you will have less control, although you can guide them on what to capture (as well as keeping them in the conversation).

Writing at speed can be tricky, so here are three tips to help you master it quickly. . .

1. Summarise what you hear. This doesn't mean apply a different interpretation but simply reduce the content to a few words that can be easily understood when read back later. Here's an example. . .

2. Work out whether you write more legibly in lower or upper case. This depends very much on your own preference. I always write in CAPITAL letters because my writing is much tidier and means it can be easily understood by the group. Some may think that writing in capital letters is a little 'shouty' but if it serves the group's understanding it is a good thing.

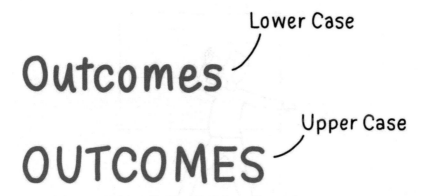

3. Writing text on a chart so it appears straight isn't always easy, especially at speed, and on occasions text can appear to be sloping off at a downward angle. The reason for this is often the way one is standing when writing on the chart. Quite often we stand to the right or the left of the chart when writing, so the group can see the text emerge. This is a good practice; however it is acceptable to stand in front of the chart briefly whilst you write if it means a tidier result, *and* if you give the group time to absorb what you have written.

There are two methods of reducing slopes. Firstly, and the quicker method, find a flipchart that is printed on squared paper. These are available and it makes writing so much easier. In the absence of squared paper you can draw in faint pencil lines if that helps.

The second method is to be aware of your posture when you are writing. Stand facing the flipchart in a central position, spread your feet slightly and bend your knees to allow your upper body to move from left to right as you write. It works and gives you a low impact workout too.

A NOTE ABOUT THE PERSON WHO WRITES NICELY

Is this you? Are you the person who, in a meeting, often gets asked to write the points on the flipchart because 'you have really nice writing'? When in the role of meeting leader please consider the person who accepts the job of working on the flipchart (often called a scribe), not because this is a particularly difficult job, but because the person at the flipchart can be at risk of being excluded from the conversation. This may not be a challenge if the person you have asked to scribe has been brought in solely for this purpose, but if your scribe is a meeting participant, and as such immersed in the meeting content, they may have a valuable contribution to make which is being missed.

PREPARATION PREPARATION PREPARATION (NOT 'WAFF WAFF WAFF')

Have you participated in a meeting where the meeting leader or facilitator, rather like the Maverick, arrives at the meeting venue unprepared and starts to 'waff on' looking for pens and creating flipcharts? I think you'll agree this is not a pretty sight, especially if everyone has arrived on time and wants to get started.

Waff (Verb):

To not achieve anything and make a lot of fuss and noise doing it. (To 'waff')
'They waff on at the start of every meeting.'

Source: The Facilitation Partnership, 2018

Preparing diligently can be a challenge of course, particularly when there are many tasks on the to-do list, but in essence the way you treat your meeting participants should be no different to how you wish to be treated as a participant yourself. Sounds simple, but it makes complete sense.

- Ask your meeting participants to describe their hopes and expectations for the meeting, which will help you plan and design the meeting itself.
- Allow yourself time to plan and prepare for your meeting away from everyday distractions.
- Use the Meet with Impact Planner to think through your meeting stage by stage, considering what participants will be doing and the tools you will use in each stage.
- Invite your participants to the meeting, clearly explaining the meeting's purpose, and expectations of them.
- Gather and prepare the visual tools and kit you need for the meeting.
- Arrive at the meeting venue no later than 30 minutes beforehand, so you can arrange the room and set up the working space in such a way that it supports the conversation.
- Allow 30 minutes for closing down the meeting space. How you leave the space will have an impact on the effectiveness of the next meeting after yours.

REFLECTING ON THE DECK

All the tools explained in Section 6 are intended to be used by groups on flipcharts or large sheets of paper. I have taken this approach deliberately in the knowledge that the use of technology to present visual information (particularly slide decks) is commonplace; however working organically in an analogue format (pen and paper) is hugely more productive because participants can physically create the information and be in the room with it.

There are many books available that will help you to hone your skills in slide presentations, and if I had included a guide here this book would probably have been twice the size. There is certainly a place for slide presentations in many meetings; however in my experience meeting leaders often use slides as a default choice for sharing information, rather than thinking about sharing in a way that could be more productive. Take a look at the Knowledge Zone (Tool 12) as an alternative approach.

If I were to provide one tip on giving slide presentations in meetings it would be 'less is more'. Fewer slides, fewer bullets, fewer long sentences and fewer complex numbers. Note that I have not said 'don't give presentations at all', which is probably unfeasible. There is absolutely a place for slide decks as pre-reads, and many people are likely to prefer them to long text-based reports. My point is that meetings are precious opportunities to collaborate, and I challenge anyone to demonstrate that long, complex slide presentations are collaborative.

I have also been thinking about technology and virtual meetings, which we explored in Section 4, but beyond the platforms that are commonly used in meetings to bring people together. Advances in tablet technology enable anyone with the right kit to lead meetings virtually using a very different approach to slide presentations.

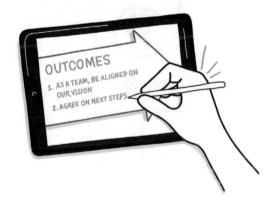

Take the iPad Pro, for example (other tablets are available), originally launched by Apple in 2015 and later accompanied by the Apple Pencil. It is possible to link your iPad into a meeting platform and use it to capture the dialogue in the meeting, for example using a mind-mapping approach (Tool 13) or even a simple list so that others on the call can see it. Remember I suggested in Section 4 that you ask someone to take the notes for you. It's a bonus if you know someone with a tablet who can do this whilst you lead the meeting.

NO PARKING

I am not a big fan of the meeting 'car park'. It is generally a dull, unloved, costly place that is easy to forget and hard to find when one wishes to return to it. The car park is often suggested as a place to note anything that is not directly relevant to the topic being discussed, so that the points do not get missed. The sad reality is that in many meetings the car park does get missed and forgotten, and the items on the chart are treated as second-class ideas behind which there is little energy to follow through because responsibility for them is unclear.

In Section 2 I urged you to be brave with your visual information choices, and I propose that you never use a car park chart again. Why? Because if the information is relevant to the meeting it will play a central role in your discussion. If a car park is suggested your response as meeting leader will be to positively recognise the suggestion and encourage the group to record any additional points themselves and commit to following up after the meeting. Whilst this is plainly not a visual approach, it is focussed on fostering a culture of initiative and responsibility.

ARE YOU BORED WITH THE BOARD TABLE?

Many times I've heard grumblings about big, heavy board tables and how their presence in a meeting room can seriously detract from the tone and productivity of the meeting. I tend to agree in many cases; however I notice that with the progression of meeting technology many such tables are increasingly wired to accommodate audio/video conferencing technology, which makes them even more immovable than before. The answer? If you can't beat them – join them!

Instead of viewing the board table as an obstruction, see it as a potential focal point for the group work by covering it in paper and using it as a surface on which to work. I've done this many times and I rather like the 'war room' feel, especially when the group has a particularly challenging problem to overcome or opportunity to exploit. Naturally you will need to adapt your meeting design to account for how the group will work around this table (and the walls around it too). Alternatively you could use the table as the Knowledge Zone (Tool 12), a central point where all the group(s) come to in order to obtain vital information.

THE GOLDEN NUGGETS

- A well-designed chart does not automatically lead to a productive meeting.
- Get to know your pen's characteristics, and what it can do for you.
- Consider the scribe: what role are they playing in your meeting?
- Using slide decks? Less is much, much more.
- Be brave: ditch the car park and encourage responsibility.
- Make the most of your meeting space. There's probably more opportunity in the room than you initially thought.

Add your own golden nuggets, insights and inspiration here. . .

MAKING IMPACT HAPPEN – 40 ESSENTIAL VISUAL TOOLS THAT BELONG TO YOU

HOW THE TOOLS ARE ORGANISED

In Section 5 I introduced you to the five stages of a successful meeting. Here they are below as a reminder.

OPENING   **WORKING**   **STRETCHING**   **DECIDING**   **MOVING**

The tools in Section 6 are purposely arranged into five groups, matching these five stages. That being said, it is possible to use a tool from one stage in another stage should it support your process. You might also choose to use a tool more than once in your meeting. For example, lists are commonly used several times in many meetings to great effect.

All the tools are deliberately simple in design and easy to create given that your time is precious. I urge you to use colour when creating your charts and embellish with simple imagery if appropriate. You will be surprised at the positive feedback you receive from your participants, and at the difference this way of working will lead to in your meetings.

Each tool has been numbered so you can refer to it quickly in your planning. Also included is a simple illustration of the tool: (1) its blank form which is intended to be a sample guide to what the tool might look like so you can create it easily, and (2) what the tool might look like once participants have used it in a meeting. Some of the tools don't use charts at all, but you'll spot those easily as you peruse. Also, in the description of the tools you will find. . .

Overview

A brief introduction to the tool and why it is used.

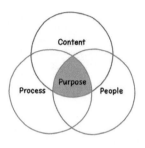

The Meeting Kaleidoscope

The strength of the tool based on People, Process and Content.

Flow flavour

I like a nice 'juicy' process, and I have suggested one for each tool. Of course, you can choose to adapt it to better suit the group's needs.

Watch out!

Things to be aware of either before or when using this tool. These might not arise, but it is worthwhile being prepared.

Resources and kit

The core materials you will need to bring this tool to life. More information is given about these in Section 5.

Expert insight

An expert tip from Ben, Catherine, Helen or me based on our experience of using this tool.

MEET THE EXPERTS

I'd like to introduce you to three very special people. I am introducing them to you now as, when you turn to the tools, you will notice that they offer insights and tips, and share their knowledge of these tools with you in the spirit of helping you and your organisation to work smarter. Meet Ben, Catherine and Helen (oh, and me too as I have added my insights against two of the tools).

Ben Robinson

Catherine Hennessy

Helen Chapman

Tom Russell

IT'S NOT WHAT YOU DO, IT'S THE WAY THAT YOU DO IT

The tools will give their absolute best if you (as meeting leader) take an active role in guiding your meeting participants through the process of using the tools. In crude terms, a good meeting leader won't use the tools simply as a data-filling exercise. The quality of the conversation is the most important element.

A great meeting leader will use the tools as a means to achieve the meeting outcomes. That's not to say that standing back and allowing the group to work is a bad thing, quite the opposite. A great meeting leader also knows when to step back and allow the conversation to develop and the group to work together.

THE MEET WITH IMPACT PLANNER

I have provided you with a visual planning tool – The Meet with Impact Planner – that you can use when planning your meetings. The design is deliberately simple so you can replicate it many times and get used to using it, and features space for the following core elements:

USING THE MEET WITH IMPACT PLANNER

The Meet with Impact Planner can be used for a short meeting with only one topic under discussion, or for a longer meeting with several topics. You will remember that Process, within the Meeting Kaleidoscope, is focussed on **how** the group works through an agenda topic, which is why you should consider all five stages for each agenda item.

The following steps will help you as you work through the process:

1. Populate the title of the meeting, the date, start and finish time, and location. It's fine if you don't know the timing at this stage, as your process thinking may lead you to a different duration than you originally anticipated.
2. Add the meeting purpose and expected outcomes. Keeping these visible will guide you as you plan the stages of the meeting.
3. Include the names of the participants whom you wish to invite.
4. Start with the first topic you wish to discuss and use the five stages of a successful meeting as your guide. Not every meeting will include all five stages; in fact many meetings don't include the Stretching stage.
5. Remember to plan your Opening stage especially well, however short or long your meeting, as this will ensure participants are focussed and ready to get to work.
6. Add the headline of conversations you wish to have about the topic at each stage, bearing in mind the intent of each stage. Using small sticky notes can be helpful instead of writing directly onto the planner, as you can move the headlines around before settling on your final design.

THE MEET WITH IMPACT PLANNER

Meeting Title:			Date:	Time:	Location:

Meeting Purpose:	Expected Outcomes:

OPENING	WORKING	STRETCHING	DECIDING	MOVING

Participants:	The Meeting Kaleidoscope:	**Purpose:** why this meeting in needed **Content:** the subjects under discussion **Process:** how you will hold your conversation **People:** the collective brains in the room

7. Note the numbers of the tools you wish to use at each stage, so you are ready to go straight to each tool page and use the examples as a guide when creating your tools.
8. Use the planner as a guide when leading your meeting. You can add timings to each stage to guide you.

The planning tool is intended to be YOUR planning tool, as the meeting leader. It is not designed to be the document you share with your meeting participants before the meeting. Use the e-mail template in Section 3 to guide you when creating a meeting invite.

Please also be mindful that just because you have planned your meeting in this way it does not always mean that your meeting will stick fast to that plan. Although you will surely be very proud of your meeting plan, resist being 'married' to it. Be prepared to adapt in the moment and make those subtle metaphorical twists and turns of the kaleidoscope as you lead your meeting.

Meet with Impact Planner – Example 1

This planner maps out a straightforward meeting that does not contain a Stretching stage. Many meetings do not contain this stage, which is completely fine, because if they did people would probably be reluctant to attend!

In addition to the important meeting purpose and outcomes you can see that the meeting leader has mapped out the start and finish time of the meeting, and where the tools will be used in each of the stages. Details of participants are also added so when it comes to sending out the invitation to the meeting everything that is needed for the e-mail is here on the planner.

THE MEET WITH IMPACT PLANNER

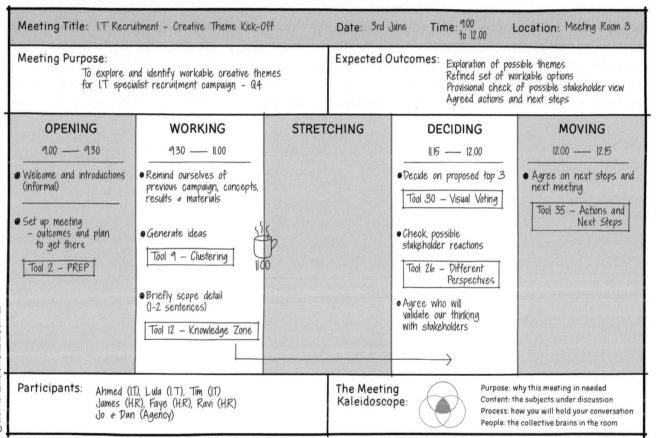

Meeting Title: IT Recruitment - Creative Theme Kick-Off   Date: 3rd June   Time: 9.00 to 12.00   Location: Meeting Room 3

Meeting Purpose:
To explore and identify workable creative themes for IT specialist recruitment campaign - Q4

Expected Outcomes:
Exploration of possible themes
Refined set of workable options
Provisional check of possible stakeholder view
Agreed actions and next steps

OPENING	WORKING	STRETCHING	DECIDING	MOVING
9.00 — 9.30	9.30 — 11.00		11.15 — 12.00	12.00 — 12.15

OPENING
- Welcome and introductions (informal)
- Set up meeting – outcomes and plan to get there

Tool 2 - PREP

WORKING
- Remind ourselves of previous campaign, concepts, results & materials
- Generate ideas

Tool 9 – Clustering

- Briefly scope detail (1-2 sentences)

Tool 12 – Knowledge Zone

11.00

DECIDING
- Decide on proposed top 3

Tool 30 – Visual Voting

- Check possible stakeholder reactions

Tool 26 – Different Perspectives

- Agree who will validate our thinking with stakeholders

MOVING
- Agree on next steps and next meeting

Tool 35 – Actions and Next Steps

Participants: Ahmed (IT), Lula (I.T), Tim (IT) James (H.R), Faye (H.R), Ravi (H.R) Jo & Dan (Agency)

The Meeting Kaleidoscope:
Purpose: why this meeting in needed
Content: the subjects under discussion
Process: how you will hold your conversation
People: the collective brains in the room

Meet with Impact Planner – Example 2

This second example features a more complex agenda over one day, including the Stretching phase, for two key topics. Again all the key information has been mapped out. For example, note how the meeting leader has indicated where the Actions and Next Steps tool has been used throughout the meeting, following Helen's tip for Tool 35.

You can see how the meeting leader has mapped out all five stages for each of the two topics. If you are holding a meeting with several topics you could use one page of the planner for each topic, so you have sight of all the visual tools you will be using throughout.

THE MEET WITH IMPACT PLANNER

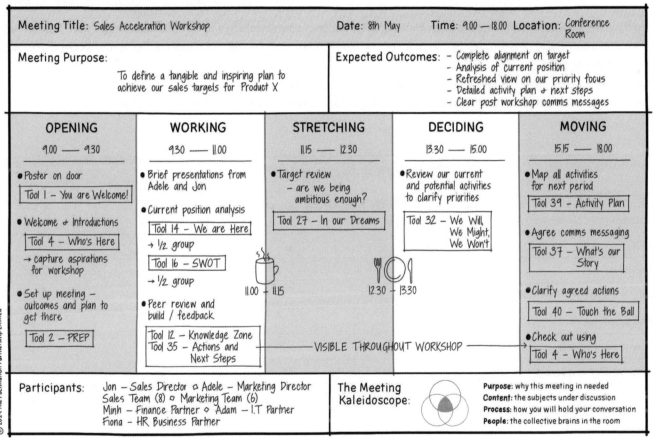

Meeting Title: Sales Acceleration Workshop   **Date:** 8th May   **Time:** 9.00 — 18.00   **Location:** Conference Room

Meeting Purpose:
To define a tangible and inspiring plan to achieve our sales targets for Product X

Expected Outcomes:
- Complete alignment on target
- Analysis of current position
- Refreshed view on our priority focus
- Detailed activity plan & next steps
- Clear post workshop comms messages

OPENING
9.00 — 9.30

- Poster on door
  - Tool 1 — You are Welcome!

- Welcome & Introductions
  - Tool 4 — Who's Here
  - → capture aspirations for workshop

- Set up meeting — outcomes and plan to get there
  - Tool 2 — PREP

WORKING
9.30 — 11.00

- Brief presentations from Adele and Jon

- Current position analysis
  - Tool 14 — We are Here
  - → 1/2 group
  - Tool 16 — SWOT
  - → 1/2 group

- Peer review and build / feedback
  - Tool 12 — Knowledge Zone
  - Tool 35 — Actions and Next Steps

11.00 — 11.15

STRETCHING
11.15 — 12.30

- Target review
  - are we being ambitious enough?
  - Tool 27 — In our Dreams

12.30 — 13.30

DECIDING
13.30 — 15.00

- Review our current and potential activities to clarify priorities
  - Tool 32 — We Will, We Might, We Won't

MOVING
15.15 — 18.00

- Map all activities for next period
  - Tool 39 — Activity Plan

- Agree comms messaging
  - Tool 37 — What's our Story

- Clarify agreed actions
  - Tool 40 — Touch the Ball

- Check out using
  - Tool 4 — Who's Here

VISIBLE THROUGHOUT WORKSHOP

Participants: Jon — Sales Director ◇ Adele — Marketing Director
Sales Team (8) ◇ Marketing Team (6)
Minh — Finance Partner ◇ Adam — I.T Partner
Fiona — HR Business Partner

The Meeting Kaleidoscope:
Purpose: why this meeting in needed
Content: the subjects under discussion
Process: how you will hold your conversation
People: the collective brains in the room

© 2019 The Facilitation Partnership Limited

THE TOOLS!

And here they are, 40 visual tools (plus the Meet with Impact Planner of course) which you can start using right now. Below I have listed the tools under each stage of a successful meeting. I have highlighted where each tool supports Content, People or Process within the Meeting Kaleidoscope.

I have also indicated where I believe a tool can be used in a virtual meeting (especially video conferencing). You might initially wonder how a tool can be used virtually, but it can be done with the help of a little creativity and lateral thinking.

Tool		Virtually possible	Content	Process	People
Stage 1 – OPENING					
1	You are Welcome!	✔			✔
2	PREP	✔	✔	✔	✔
3	Mugshot	✔			✔
4	Who's Here?	✔			✔
5	The Essence of. . .	✔			✔
6	3 Word Introduction	✔			✔
7	Helped and Hindered	✔	✔	✔	✔
8	Gives and Gets	✔			✔

Tool		Virtually possible	Content	Process	People
Stage 2 – WORKING					
9	Clustering		✔		
10	Graffiti Wall	✔	✔		
11	'It's easy, what you do is. . . '	✔	✔		
12	Knowledge Zone	✔	✔		
13	Mind Map	✔	✔	✔	
14	'We are here' (PEST)	✔	✔	✔	
15	Process Map	✔	✔		
16	SWOT	✔	✔		
17	Timeline	✔	✔		✔
18	Inspiration Filter	✔	✔	✔	
19	GROW	✔	✔	✔	
20	Human Cluster		✔		✔

Tool		Virtually possible	Content	Process	People
Stage 3 – STRETCHING					
21	Journey/Transition Map	✔	✔		
22	Push and Pull	✔	✔		
23	'There is never any milk!'	✔	✔	✔	
24	Picture Cards	✔	✔		✔
25	Enhanced Idea	✔	✔	✔	
26	Different Perspectives	✔	✔		✔
27	In Our Dreams	✔	✔		
28	Why? Why? Why? Why? Why?	✔	✔	✔	

Tool		Virtually possible	Content	Process	People
Stage 4 – DECIDING					
29	Two by Two	✔	✔	✔	
30	Visual Voting	✔		✔	
31	Show Me the Money!	✔		✔	
32	We Will, We Might, We Won't	✔	✔	✔	
33	Thinking Hats	✔	✔	✔	

Tool		Virtually possible	Content	Process	People
Stage 5 – MOVING					
34	Needs and Offers	✔	✔		✔
35	Actions and Next Steps	✔	✔		
36	My Best Advice	✔			✔
37	What's Our Story?	✔	✔		
38	Letter to Me	✔	✔		✔
39	Activity Plan	✔	✔		
40	Touch the Ball		✔		✔

OPENING

☐1 YOU ARE WELCOME!

Overview

The purpose of this tool is to do just that, welcome your participants to the meeting. Your poster doesn't need to be complex or particularly artistic, unless you want it to be. Placing your poster either on the door of the meeting room or just outside will orientate your participants to the right room. It might even be the start of your own meeting brand!

The Meeting Kaleidoscope

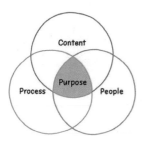

A great tool for making your participants feel included and part of something special, even before they have entered the room. Consider who your participants are and whether any particular imagery or colour might be especially attractive or topical.

Flow flavour

1. Make sure you've placed the poster in good time before participants arrive.
2. If your meeting is one of a series on the same subject or with the same group of participants, consider a common theme for each poster.

Watch out!

If your meeting is confidential, or likely to be sensitive, place the poster just inside the room, for example on a flipchart easel, so it can be easily seen when participants enter.

Resources and kit

A sheet of flipchart paper, marker pens and tape.

Catherine's expert insight

'This tool is super-speedy and simple to execute yet delivers a multitude of positive subliminal messages to the people taking part in your meeting. It's a little like going to a formal meal and finding a handwritten card with your name on it in your place-setting. You feel expected, thought about, valued and welcome at the table. This simple tool can do a lot of work on your behalf, supporting you in establishing trust and confidence within the group and supporting you in creating a truly welcoming environment.'

2 PREP

Overview

If there's a tool that can be used in absolutely every meeting – it's PREP. This tool is not only used at the outset to focus your participants on what's to be achieved and how, but it forms a regular check-in point during your meeting to check you are on-track. For some this could be described as an agenda chart, but it's much, much more than that.

PREP is divided into four key areas. These are:

1. **P**urpose for being here (why does this meeting need to happen?)
2. How we will use our **R**esources (including the brains in the room, roles and how we will work: for example is the meeting a combination of presentation and group working etc.?)
3. Our **E**xpected outcomes (what we aim to achieve by the end of the meeting)
4. Our **P**lan to get there (the key conversations we need to have).

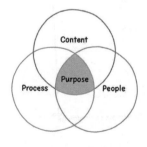

The Meeting Kaleidoscope

This tool represents an intersection of People, Content and Process, centred around the Purpose as described in the Meeting Kaleidoscope.

Flow flavour

1. Prepare a chart using the example illustration for inspiration. Ideally all sections should be on one chart so they can be viewed together, but if you need to create on more than one flipchart that will also work well.
2. Clearly position the chart in the room so that all participants can see it at all times during the meeting.
3. Starting with the Purpose, remind your participants why this meeting is taking place (they will know this from the meeting invitation), then move to expected outcomes, and the plan to get there. Finally, agree with the group about how it intends to work. For example, there may be different roles being played in the room, and it is recommended that you draw attention to these at the outset to avoid surprises later.
4. Check with the group for clarification on the PREP chart before moving into the next stage of your meeting, and respond to any questions they may have.
5. Refer back to the chart during your meeting as a way of helping participants to understand where they are in the meeting plan. Do this sparingly, at key points such as after breaks, lunch and at the end of the meeting.
6. Take a photo of the chart at the end of the meeting and send to participants (alongside other chart photos) to clearly remind them of the conversation.

JUICY

Watch out!

- You will have communicated the purpose and expected outcomes to your participants before your meeting, so they are clear about why they are attending and what's to be achieved. Make sure your chart mirrors the previous description, as significant differences may cause confusion.
- Never take the PREP chart down or cover it during the meeting. It should act as an important focal point throughout the conversation.

Resources and kit

A large sheet of flipchart paper, a good range of coloured marker pens, tape and ruler/straight edge.

Helen's expert insight

'Can you make a direct connection between your meeting and the purpose of your organisation? If you can't explain the connection (out loud) to somebody clearly and simply, you should think twice about why you're having the meeting.

It's easy to fall into the trap of 'meetings for meetings' sake.' We get sucked into a maelstrom of competing priorities and it seems sensible to put yet another meeting in the diary just to keep up.

I wonder when does the work get done? People tell me they arrive at work earlier and stay later to do the work they couldn't do because their day was spent in meetings! Like running hard only to stand still; a lot of energy is expended, but for what real value?

PREP is a simple framework that will help you achieve clarity: Why this meeting? Why these people? Why now?

Notice that Purpose, Resources and Expected Outcomes come before the Plan (the agenda). That's because an agenda without a clear foundation can end up being a random list of things to discuss. PRE provides clear focus and gives P substance and reason.

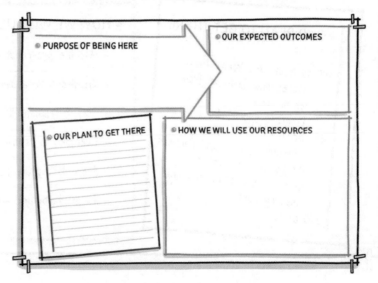

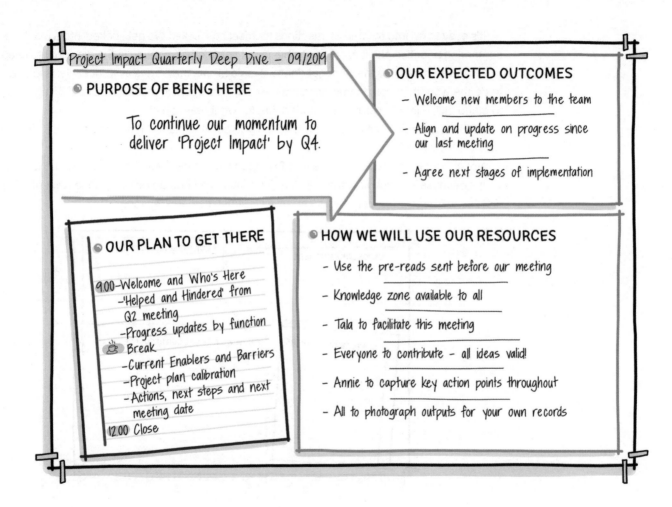

Project Impact Quarterly Deep Dive – 09/2019

PURPOSE OF BEING HERE

To continue our momentum to deliver 'Project Impact' by Q4.

OUR EXPECTED OUTCOMES

- Welcome new members to the team

- Align and update on progress since our last meeting

- Agree next stages of implementation

OUR PLAN TO GET THERE

9.00 – Welcome and Who's Here
  – 'Helped and Hindered' from Q2 meeting
  – Progress updates by function
Break
  – Current Enablers and Barriers
  – Project plan calibration
  – Actions, next steps and next meeting date
12.00 Close

HOW WE WILL USE OUR RESOURCES

- Use the pre-reads sent before our meeting

- Knowledge zone available to all

- Tala to facilitate this meeting

- Everyone to contribute – all ideas valid!

- Annie to capture key action points throughout

- All to photograph outputs for your own records

3 MUGSHOT

Overview

A fun visual activity designed to help participants get to know each other and feel comfortable. This tool is based on the idea that most people have a favourite mug used for their coffee or tea at work, and usually everyone knows to whom each mug belongs. This tool will help develop a sense of each participant's character as they design a fictional mug that tells other participants about them.

The Meeting Kaleidoscope

Very much focussed on people in the early stages of your meeting. A good tool to use to get participants ready for visual working later in the meeting.

Flow flavour

1. Provide one sheet of flipchart paper for each participant. Smaller sheets of paper are also great if you have less space in which to work.
2. Ideally, you will have drawn a blank mug on each sheet beforehand, so the image takes up as much space on the paper as possible. Alternatively you could ask participants to draw the mug outline themselves, copying a template you have prepared. Even drawing the mug itself can be an amusing experience.

3. Ensure participants have access to a range of coloured markers, the more colours the better, and ask participants to create a design on their mug that tells others about them. This could be their interests, or maybe a statement.
4. Allow approximately 10 minutes, and ask participants to present their mugs to each other and explain why they have chosen their specific design. Encourage others to ask questions.

Watch out!

If you are leading a large group, guide participants to be concise in their explanation of their mug if you are short of time, or simply encourage a 'gallery walk' whereby participants take a walk around the room and look at each other's work.

Resources and kit

Flipchart paper (or slightly smaller), a good range of coloured marker pens and tape.

Tom's expert insight

'What I love about this tool is the fun it brings to the group through something very simple. Even if people don't have a specific mug at work most can identify with owning something that tells everyone about their personality. I've used this exercise with clients who I know have their own 'mug culture', and the advantage of the mug is that it is often found in the office, where meetings are usually held. What other items can you think of that might be relevant to the meeting you are leading, which could serve as a fun way of getting to know each other?'

4 WHO'S HERE?

Overview

Who's Here? is a simple tool designed to generate a sense of mutual trust and help participants feel comfortable as they start the meeting. The tool is based on a simple circular theme, with a central 'Who's here?' point (or any other title you wish to use, such as the name of the meeting) and a number of segments fanning out from the centre, rather like sunbeams, matching the number of meeting participants.

    An advantage of using this tool is that you can refer back to it at the end of your meeting. For example, if you ask your participants what they wish to get out of the meeting you can return to it to check whether they achieved their aim.

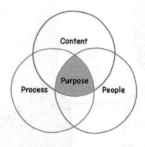

The Meeting Kaleidoscope

Whilst primarily focussed on participants and who they are, this tool can signpost individual aspirations if you draw the group's attention to the meeting purpose.

Flow flavour

1. Draw up your centre point and segments in advance of the meeting, assuming you know how many people will be attending. When ready to start, have several colour markers ready (use the tip in Section 5 to keep your marker pens together).
2. Invite each participant to introduce themselves by their name, and other information you would like to know. For example, you may want to find out the function they work in, what their big hope is for this meeting, or maybe a fact that other participants may not be aware of.
3. Record the responses yourself, or ask someone to do that for you. Aim to use one colour for each category of information, which will make it easier to distinguish content.
4. When completed, keep the chart visible so participants, and you, can refer to it throughout the meeting. Return to the chart at the end of the meeting as appropriate.

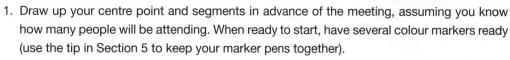

Watch out!

- Asking for too much information can lead to a very messy chart. Keep it to two to three simple points, and summarise when you capture the information.
- If you have a larger group, you may wish to use a larger sheet of paper.

Resources and kit

A sheet of flipchart paper, three to four cool colour pens, plus one 'hot' colour for highlighting and tape.

Catherine's expert insight

'This simple visual way of working serves many purposes for you in a meeting. It gives you a great data reference point to work with and add to, a low-risk way of giving everyone the opportunity to speak and by its visual structure demonstrates:

1. that everybody is welcomed and expected as an important part of the meeting
2. everybody is expected to share their view and play an active role in the meeting
3. the group share a common bond.

Not bad for a simple poster! Genius!'

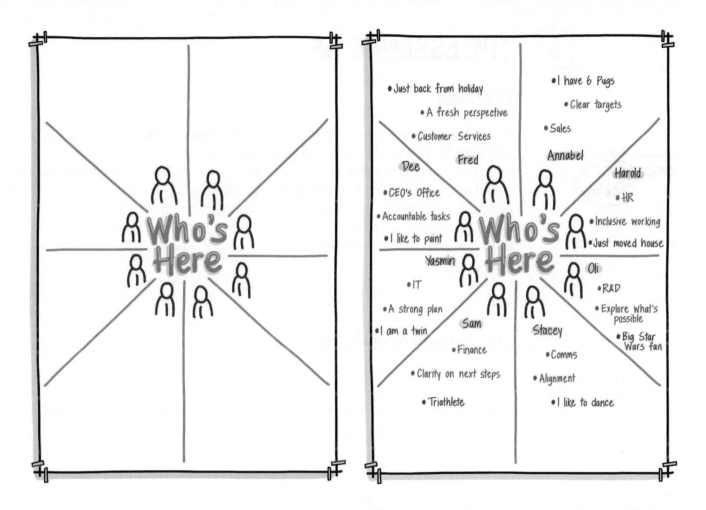

5 | THE ESSENCE OF...

Overview

For many participants sharing information about themselves can be an engaging activity. We all tend to like talking about ourselves and we're probably the best person to do it too. The Essence of... is designed to be highly versatile, and uses visual materials to communicate the essence of someone to others. This tool will help your participants to become comfortable with others, particularly if you have people of different hierarchical levels in the meeting.

The Essence of... could also be used in other stages of your meeting, such as to stretch thinking and encourage conversation about a concept or idea that might otherwise be difficult to articulate.

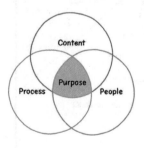

The Meeting Kaleidoscope

This tool 'opens the window' on fellow participants, highlighting things they enjoy as people rather than as leaders, managers and colleagues in a work setting. This can lead to an eye-opening conversation at times, so be prepared to learn things you may not have expected!

Flow flavour

1. Before the meeting, ask your participants to bring with them an image that conveys the essence of themselves. This can be a photograph or image that a participant can easily explain to the group. For example, a participant may choose to share a photo of them and their family, an image of a hobby, their favourite book, or a photo of their new car. Whatever it is will be the right image to choose, as everyone is gloriously different.
2. Invite each participant to share their image that conveys the essence of them. Encourage them to explain why it has been chosen and allow other participants to ask questions if needed.
3. Give everyone the chance to share, and thank everyone for their contribution.
4. You may wish to display the images around the room during the meeting as a reminder of how different we all are.

Watch out!

- Remember to give plenty of notice to participants when requesting the image.
- In the case of photographs it may be wise to encourage photocopies to be brought into the meeting rather than the originals, especially if they are precious.

Resources and kit

Printed images (provided by participants) and tape.

Helen's expert insight

'Whenever using a tool like this, it is important to explain why so that the group see the connection between the purpose of the meeting and the essence they are sharing about themselves. For example, when using The Essence of. . . in a group of people meeting for the first time it is best to ask them to share their 'get to know me essence'. In contrast, with a group who have known each other longer, it is possible to ask them to share their 'when I'm tired essence' or 'what you may not know about me yet essence'. Whichever angle you choose, explain to the group why sharing their essence will benefit the work to be done together.'

6 | 3 WORD INTRODUCTION

Overview

The 3 Word Introduction is a very simple tool, which can be used visually or not depending upon the resources you have available, although taking a visual approach will help participants to absorb the information more effectively than using a verbal approach alone.

   This tool is a powerful method of encouraging participants to get to know and understand one another, and using it at the beginning of your meeting will help to develop a sense of community and trust within the group.

   You can also choose different topics for the three words, for example you might ask participants to describe how they are feeling right now, what they are most looking forward to in the meeting, or what's important to them about the topic to be discussed – the choice is yours.

The Meeting Kaleidoscope

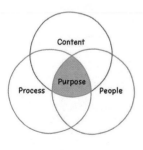

Great at highlighting the current mood or thinking of participants. Not only a strong way of getting to know each other better but potentially a useful barometer for the meeting leader to sense how participants are feeling or the common thoughts the group have.

Flow flavour

1. Provide participants with a sheet of paper and a marker pen.
2. Ask each participant to write down the three words that reflect the question you have asked, for example 'Describe how you are feeling right now in three words'.
3. Allow participants the opportunity to write down their three words on the paper.
4. If energy is lower, invite participants to stand up together and share whilst standing.
5. In any order, ask participants to share their three words with the group. You will find that other participants will comment and enjoy what has been offered.
6. When everyone has offered their words, thank the group and summarise the essence of what has been shared. For example: 'There seems to be real energy right now, let's unleash it on our first topic for exploration!'
7. Display the words on the wall or around the room if appropriate.

Watch out!

No significant watch outs here, it's all good!

Resources and kit

Paper (e.g., photocopying size) and marker pens.

Helen's expert insight

'In three words. . .
Helps Focus Brains
Connect to PREP
Give Thinking Time
No Judging Please
Every Contribution Welcome
Repeat at Intervals
Easy Yet Powerful.'

7 | HELPED AND HINDERED

Overview

The purpose of Helped and Hindered is to reflect on what helped or hindered a meeting in achieving its desired outcomes, so that participants can learn from the insights shared and contribute to a more productive meeting either now or in the future. One option is to use this chart in the Opening stage of your meeting, inviting participants to think back to the previous meeting. This works well if you have regular meetings and the time between them is short. Alternatively, this tool could be used in the Moving stage of your meeting, harnessing the group's thinking whilst it is fresh.

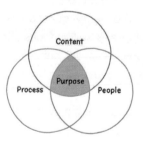

The Meeting Kaleidoscope

I have highlighted all three elements of the Meeting Kaleidoscope here as this tool allows meeting participants to explore their thoughts on the previous meeting, which could include all three areas, and indeed the meeting purpose too.

Flow flavour

1. Prepare your flipchart templates using the example illustration as inspiration.
2. Explain the purpose of the process to the group, emphasising that the focus is on an objective view of the meeting in service of making the next meeting even better.
3. Start with either Helped or Hindered, and keep to one section before moving to the other. To ensure that you get everybody's best thinking ask people to make their own notes of any points that they will want to raise later as you move to the other section.
4. Invite participants to call out their observations, noting them on the chart as you progress (or ask someone to do that for you). Encourage participants to offer specific observations, rather than general comments. Five to 10 minutes should be ample for this conversation.
5. When everyone has had a chance to contribute move to the other half, again encouraging suggestions. Lead the process at a swift and steady pace.
6. Encourage the group to seek clarity if there are any points that are unclear.
7. Now that you have all your content, use your second chart to pose the question 'So what will we do more of/differently at our next meeting?' Add emphasis to 'will' to focus attention.
8. Again, encourage the group to be specific in their suggestions, which will help everyone to understand what is being requested. Make sure these points are captured on the chart. This should take approximately 5 to 10 minutes.
9. Draw the group's attention to the whole set of suggestions, and seek agreement from the group to make these a reality.

Watch out!

- It is possible that participants may want to debate an observation about what helped or hindered the last meeting. Of course if you have time this may be useful; however this tool is focussed on making things work even better in the future rather than reviewing the details.
- If you have participants who are quieter (or louder) than others, get participants to write their suggestions on sticky notes in silence instead of calling out their views. This will encourage everyone to contribute equally.
- Should you choose to use this tool at the end of your meeting, be aware that participants may offer superficial answers due to tiredness or a desire to finish, in which case use the tool as a brief 'sweeping up' exercise to capture comments quickly and then refer to them at the beginning of your next meeting when people have the energy to do some quality work.

Resources and kit

Flipchart, marker pens and tape.

Ben's expert insight

'This simple tool has multiple direct and indirect benefits but the overwhelming motive for me is *continuity*. Using this in the Opening stage of your meetings will connect people to the previous meeting. What did we achieve? What were the outputs? Have we progressed? It will help them to evaluate and see the value whilst also identifying where there are missed opportunities and improvements.

Running the tool in the Closing stage of the meeting will enable you to use that data and look for continuity whilst planning the next meeting.

Bonus tip – this is a handy tool when reviewing *nearly anything*, not just meetings!'

 **HELPED**

 **HINDERED**

HELPED	HINDERED
→ We kept to time	→ We could have all read the pre-reads
→ We focussed on the really important topics	→ Our guest was late
→ We gave ourselves time to break	→ The sales report should have been sent around earlier
→ We reflected on how we worked AND the work we did	→ Start time could have been later to account for traffic
→ The room was light and spacious	

8 GIVES AND GETS

Overview

Gives and Gets is an effective tool that draws attention to both what participants bring to the meeting (or give to others), including knowledge, expertise and perspective, and what they wish to get out of the meeting itself, thus creating a sense of balance and mutuality. Remember the intersection where diversity of thinking creates super conditions for innovation? This tool will highlight these differences well, encouraging participants to make the most of the 'brains in the room'.

This tool can be run with or without sticky notes. I have explained a process below which includes sticky notes, although you can simply capture the points on a flipchart.

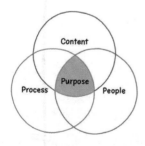

The Meeting Kaleidoscope

Focused on people for the benefit of the people in the room. This tool is, unsurprisingly, focussed on the core element of any meeting – people!

Flow flavour

1. Prepare a flipchart, or two flipcharts, with the titles 'Give' and 'Get', using the example as inspiration.
2. Invite participants to reflect on what they bring to the meeting, including what they offer that may be unique to the group, and what they would like to get from the meeting (e.g., their 'big wish').
3. Invite someone to start, capturing their give and get headlines on the relevant area of the chart. Ask questions if any points are unclear.
4. Invite others to follow, until you have captured all suggestions.
5. Summarise the content, drawing out key themes, or where you see differences that may be important to the conversation. Or ask members of the group to offer that summary to increase their interaction and ownership.
6. Return to the chart, especially the 'Gets', at the end of the meeting as a way of checking to see whether participants all achieved their 'get'.

Watch out!

- How you frame this tool will be key. Ensure that when you refer to gives and gets (especially gives) you provide clarity on the context of the 'gives' in relation to the meeting. For example, you might ask for suggestions on what participants might bring that others don't, which may lead to responses such as 'a detailed knowledge of our information technology capability'. These types of suggestions are very different to (and far more useful than) generic responses such as 'a good sense of humour'.

- If you are using sticky notes, ensure there is enough space for all notes to be easily seen. Using separate charts may be a wise move.

Resources and kit

Flipchart, marker pens and tape. Sticky notes if required.

Ben's expert insight

'Let's be clear, everyone within any meeting room should know exactly what value they can add and what is in it for them in their job role. Sometimes this is not always clear to them or indeed to other participants in the room so it is excellent meeting practice to call it out especially if this meeting or group will continue working together afterwards.

Using this quick and handy tool in the Opening stage of the meeting lets you have that important conversation early on in a team's lifecycle. The crucial thing is to follow up on it. For example, if you feel you are missing a particular perspective in the meeting, fill the gap and find that person. If there are people who genuinely cannot find anything to offer – be generous and give them their time back.'

GIVES

GETS

GIVES

- Clarity on what I really need
- Jargon free explanations!
- My complete attention (no phone!)
- My support to make this team rock
- Challenging questions
- A 'this team is Job#1' attitude

 GETS

- Your honesty
- Your focussed attention
- Simple language please!
- Full on openness
- Commitment to tangible action
- Real momentum

WORKING

9 CLUSTERING

Overview

This tool's name essentially refers to the grouping of common ideas or concepts and is most commonly used with sticky notes. This method enables everyone to 'have a voice' and you can even use a silent clustering process, an effective way of reducing the impact that louder or more dominant participants have on their colleagues.

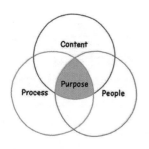

The Meeting Kaleidoscope

Clustering focusses primarily on content by allowing participants to quickly see common themes and differences in outputs.

Flow flavour

1. Prepare a large sheet of paper that will be big enough to take sticky notes generated by your meeting participants. Add your title or question to be considered or answered. For example, 'What are our values as a high performing team?'

2. Ensure all participants have access to sticky notes. Larger size sticky notes are preferable if you are expecting participants to write more than one word answers.
3. Guide individual participants to reflect on the question and note as many responses as they wish, using one sticky note per response.
4. You may also ask participants to remain silent throughout the whole process to eliminate any inappropriate influence.
5. Once all participants have written their answers and placed the sticky notes on the chart, ask the group to work as a team to cluster the responses into common themes.
6. Leading a conversation to understand the essence of each theme, if appropriate, will be helpful, especially if you need to reach agreement on a title for each group of sticky notes.

Watch out!

- This process can be used straight onto a wall if you don't have paper large enough.
- Make sure the wall surface you are using responds well to sticky notes as they can fall off, which could affect your process.

Be aware that, depending on the size of the group, you may be generating more information than people's brains can handle, or physical space allows. In which case give people time to think and decide on their top three or four.

Resources and kit

A sheet of paper (as large as possible), marker pens (thin nib), sticky notes (the bigger the better) and tape.

Helen's expert insight

'These days, we get more practice typing on a keyboard than we do writing with pen and paper. So much so that when I ask a group to write on sticky notes, they often make light-hearted jokes about their poor handwriting and spelling (we're so used to auto-correct). As the process of Clustering requires the group to read each other's writing, it works well to give a couple of tips as you set the exercise up.

Here's what I do:

- Join in with their light-heartedness to ease any shyness.
- Remind them that the exercise is about sharing ideas (all handwriting welcome and mis-spelling OK).
- Suggest they write in capital letters because these are easier to read quickly.
- Ask for one thought per sticky note.

I also find it works well to ask for short sentences that others can read quickly rather than writing single words. For example, one word (say. . . COMMUNICATION) on a sticky note could mean different things to different readers and create confusion in the group. Whereas, writing a short sentence (say. . . WE SPEAK OVER ONE ANOTHER) is less ambiguous and more helpful for the group to understand your thought.'

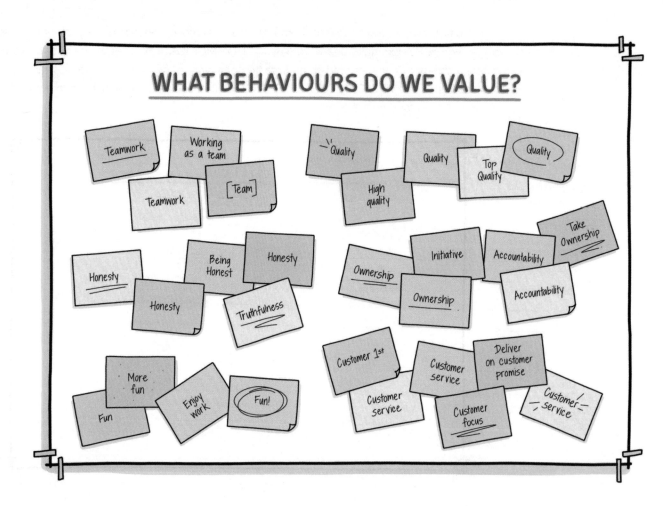

WHAT BEHAVIOURS DO WE VALUE?

⏢10⏢ GRAFFITI WALL

Overview

The Graffiti Wall is a versatile tool that can be used for many different purposes. Its simplicity also means that it can be set up in a flash, yet it can hold a range of valuable insights to support your meeting.

The Meeting Kaleidoscope

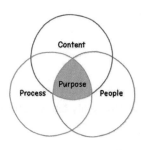

Like the Knowledge Wall, the Graffiti Wall is focussed on content, although unlike the Knowledge Wall this tool starts with a completely blank space and builds during the meeting. Graffiti walls are especially powerful in larger meetings and conferences where there are more people who could add their responses on the chart.

Flow flavour

1. Hang a large sheet of paper on the wall, the bigger the better. If you have flipchart paper consider combining them to create a larger working space. In order to maximise the chances of participants adding to the chart your wall (and pens) need to be located in a place where it can be easily seen and accessed. In the coffee area is usually a good place.

2. Add your heading to the chart, and make sure what you are asking for is completely clear. For example, 'What makes you proud to work here?'
3. Orientate participants to the wall and explain its purpose and how it will be used in the meeting. Remember to refer back to the wall from time to time to encourage participation.
4. Being the first person to write on the wall can be daunting. You may wish to ask someone if they will agree to add their response so others may follow.
5. Gather round the wall and review the content with your participants. Encourage the group to seek clarity on any content that is unclear, or explain what stands out for them.
6. Depending upon your meeting process this may feed into your subsequent conversations.

Watch out!

Participants will contribute to the Graffiti Wall if they are clear on its purpose, the question/topic in focus, and what will happen to the information after the meeting. Ambiguity and this tool tend not to mix well, so be as clear as possible with your request.

Resources and kit

A large sheet of paper (preferable), marker pens and tape.

Catherine's expert insight

'The Graffiti Wall can be an absolute game changer if it's used boldly. I have used it to great effect with large groups where it is a way to ensure that everybody's voice gets "heard". I encourage the use of the Graffiti Wall as a place to capture thoughts and ideas that are at risk of not being said out loud in a meeting. Sometimes meeting leaders are worried about giving people the opportunity to "vent" and share what they are concerned or uncomfortable with. My advice to them is that if you don't create the opportunity then dissatisfaction/confusion doesn't go away but festers and pops up in other conversations or behaviours. To make bold use of the Graffiti Wall you could put up some guiding questions such as "What are we mad about?", "What are we sad about?" and "What are we glad about?". This will get you great data that you can use to seed a meaningful conversation.'

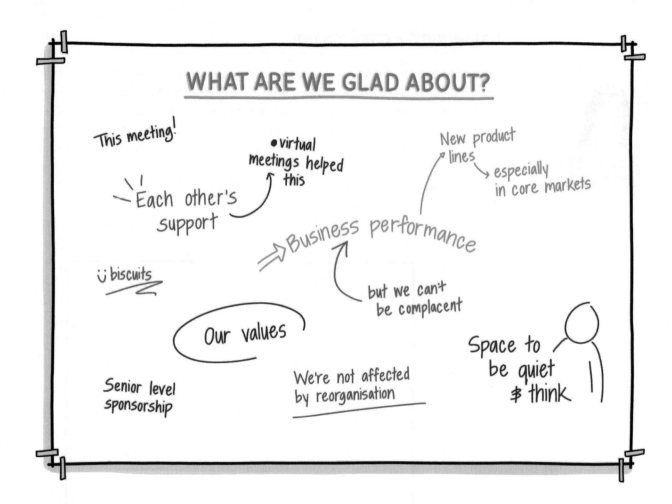

WHAT ARE WE GLAD ABOUT?

This meeting!

Each other's support

• virtual meetings helped this

New product lines → especially in core markets

→ Business performance

ツ biscuits

but we can't be complacent

Our values

Senior level sponsorship

We're not affected by reorganisation

Space to be quiet & think

11 'IT'S EASY, WHAT YOU DO IS...'

Overview

This tool is hugely powerful in its simplicity and speed to share potential ideas and suggestions. What's more, it can be facilitated as an open or closed process, which means it could yield even more innovative results and adapt itself to the way your group may find most productive.

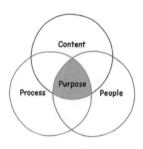

The Meeting Kaleidoscope

Fast, furious content is the focus here – unleash the inspiration!

Flow flavour

1. Prepare a flipchart or large sheet of paper with the heading 'It's easy, what you do is. . . '. Use the example illustration for inspiration.
2. Focus the group on the key question to be answered: for example 'How do I. . . ?', 'How can we. . . ?'

3. Ask each participant to provide their idea by starting off their sentence with 'What you do is. . .' and state an idea they have to offer. Once a participant has provided their idea move to the next participant and so on.
4. Repeat this process several times with all participants until sufficient ideas have been offered. If a participant does not have an idea to offer they can simply say 'Pass' and the process moves to the next participant.
5. If the question originated from a participant, ask them if they have got what they needed.

Watch out!

- Participants may want to offer all their ideas in one go. Encourage them to share one idea initially as more chances will come around.
- There may be times when participants have hugely different ideas which they may be reluctant to share because they feel their suggestion is too 'wacky' compared to others' ideas. An alternative way of running this process is to use a sheet of paper (e.g., A4) and ask participants to write their suggestion at the top of the paper and then fold over the paper and pass it to the next participant. At the end of the process you will have a sheet full of wonderful ideas. This alternative process is clearly less interactive but you may wish to have several ideas travelling around the group at the same time.

Resources and kit

Flipchart paper, marker pens and tape (or smaller sheets and pens for the alternative process).

Catherine's expert insight

'I love witnessing the quality results that arise from using this "It's easy, what you do is. . . " tool. It's deceptively simple and so powerful. When a group gets stuck or a problem seems too challenging then flipping that "stuckness" into high energy in a couple of elegant steps is a great service to offer a group. By declaring it easy and setting up a process that enables each person to offer their thinking you (a) reinforce the group's sense of their own capability and create a sense of positive achievement and (b) create a non-hierarchical, low-pressure way of gathering fresh ideas fast.

My big tip to get the best results is to set this up carefully to give it a "light" exploratory feel by ensuring the group know that there are no "wrong answers" and that all ideas are welcome. It can be very gratifying when an individual has posed a question or asked for help with a problem and can then be seen grinning because they now have more options to choose from than they could ever have created alone.'

12 KNOWLEDGE ZONE

Overview

In Section 5 I mentioned the Knowledge Zone as an example of how you can share information in a meeting without resorting to time-consuming and complex slide decks.

The purpose of the Knowledge Zone is to act as a point of information that your meeting participants can access during the meeting. How you structure and organise the Knowledge Zone is completely up to you. Documents including spreadsheets, presentations, reports, posters, plus physical products etc. are all great, providing they support the purpose of your meeting and the work you are expecting participants to undertake. Remember the different senses and how you can maximise the participant experience (e.g., touching and smelling products).

Knowledge Zones are particularly useful in meetings where participants need to access information to support their thinking, such as Meeting Scenario 2 described in Section 2.

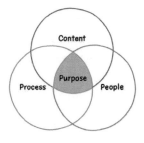

The Meeting Kaleidoscope

The Knowledge Zone is all about content. It should be your hub for all things data – both low and hi tech.

Flow flavour

1. If you need participants to contribute materials to the Knowledge Zone ensure you ask them in advance of the meeting so they have time to collate the required information/items.
2. Set up your Knowledge Zone in advance of your meeting, ensuring you have the materials needed for the group to do their work. Remember to use the space well, including the use of flat and wall surfaces in order to ensure the materials are clearly visible.
3. Explain the purpose of the Knowledge Zone to the group before they need to use it. Guide the group to use the materials in the Knowledge Zone itself and ensure there are enough copies of resources available so that people avoid having to wait to access what they need.

Watch out!

- When selecting a meeting room remember to choose one that will accommodate the Knowledge Zone and the space in which participants need to work.
- Encourage participants to use the material at the Knowledge Zone itself, rather than taking the material away. This is particularly important where you may have several groups working on similar content.

Resources and kit

A space in the meeting room with a table, ample wall space. Documents, posters, materials and tape.

Helen's expert insight

'Too much information clogs up the system, slows down discussion and can leave some people behind. Too little information can result in a loss of insight, understanding and opportunity.

It's tricky to get the balance right. It can help to think about this in terms of Push and Pull.

A Push example is the use of PowerPoint. People often get absorbed into creating a dazzling PowerPoint presentation and, in doing so, miss the opportunity to *truly engage* the assembled brains with the information and knowledge being shared. I believe that PowerPoint presentations have their place, but if people in meetings are treated like an audience, the chances are that's how they'll behave. They will mostly be passive observers who will rate you on your performance. If you have ever been met with an awkward "tumbleweed moment" after asking, "Any questions?" at the end of a PowerPoint presentation, it's a sign that you have failed to fully engage the group.

A Knowledge Zone used throughout a meeting can provide the opportunity to summarise and share insight, data, opinion (Push) *and* for people to get what they need (Pull) by using it as the basis for exploration, discussion and decision making.'

13 MIND MAP

Overview

Mind-mapping as a technique was popularised in the 1970s by Tony Buzan; however diagrams and radial maps have been used for centuries.

In a meeting context Mind Maps are a powerful method of exploring a topic and capturing granular detail in a way that flows easily.

Like the Who's Here? tool (Tool 4) the Mind Map works with a central point on the chart, which is usually the topic or question under discussion. The tool uses 'branches' that emerge from the central question, around which further detail can be added, either as further questions or additional factors to be considered.

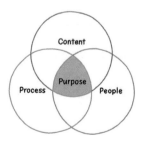

The Meeting Kaleidoscope

The Mind Map is very much aligned to content; however the mind-mapping process has a strong foundation in the process of how the information itself is added and structured.

Flow flavour

1. Add your central point to the chart, either a subject heading or question. For example, 'New product ideas'.
2. Explain that the purpose of the process is to surface all the details relevant to the question or topic.
3. If you are leading the conversation and capturing information at the same time, start with the big themes that emerge from the group, which in this case will be the ideas for a new product.
4. For each idea, add a new subheading around the central point, and attach it to the central point using a line or a branch. You may wish to use different colours for different branches.
5. You will need to make a choice whether you continue leading the group and capturing the content, or whether you wish to ask the group to work on the Mind Map. If you choose the second option consider dividing the group by the number of branches, or if it's a small group consider asking them to work on a small number of branches.
6. The next task is to add the next layer of detail to the branches, in this case writing down the characteristics of each new product idea, for example what it looks like, how it will be delivered, who the customer is. The process continues as further ideas are added and the branches get more and more detailed.
7. Once complete, encourage the group to summarise the content either as a whole tool or by branch.

Watch out!

- Mind Maps can become large and detailed. Make sure you have enough space on your chart. Flipchart paper can work, and consider using the sheet in landscape format.
- If the branches start to get close to each other it can be difficult to see which content relates to which branch. Using different colours for different branches will help.
- Summarising Mind Map content can be a long process due to the amount of content. When seeking feedback from the group try asking for the big Aha! points that stood out for them. Highlight these on the chart so they can be easily seen.
- You can also give the group members sticky dots to vote with (Tool 30) so that they can illustrate what's important to them – this makes the process more democratic and helps to prevent a situation whereby the most vocal members of the group lead the way.

Resources and kit

A large sheet of paper (preferable), marker pens (thin nib) and tape.

Ben's expert insight

'When you visualise what you are aiming to achieve here, please don't imagine a beautiful Buzan classic! I find the best Mind Maps created live in meetings are messy and have many mistakes, and as a result they will have then been created by a group, as a memory of a valuable conversation and the output can be used as a business tool and referred back to.

My top tips would be to get the group involved in its creation as much as possible and to have mentally planned a loose structure beforehand. Imagine what the big branches might be and have a sense of the topics before diving into the conversation.'

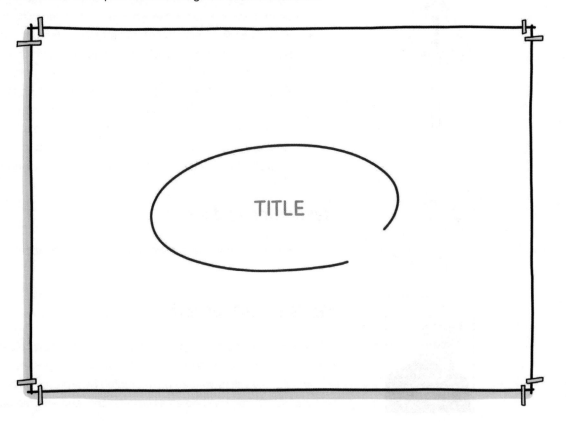

14 'WE ARE HERE' (PEST)

Overview

The 'We are here' tool uses the PEST approach (Political, Economic, Social and Technological), a long-established and insightful tool designed to help make an assessment of the surrounding environment. Later versions of the tool include PESTLE, which adds Legal and Environmental factors to the assessment.

When using this tool you don't need to stick to the PEST titles, but if you do decide to create new headings ensure they can be clearly understood by your participants.

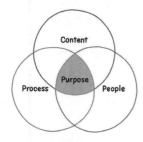

The Meeting Kaleidoscope

This tool primarily focusses on Content, supported by a robust process, by drawing together insights held by participants and assembling them in a way that starts to generate wider meaning.

Flow flavour

1. Prepare your chart using the example illustration for inspiration. You may wish to keep all four sections together on one large chart, or use a separate chart for each. This may depend upon the size of your group and the space available.

2. Orientate participants to the chart and explain the process, referring to each of the headings and what they mean for absolute clarity.
3. Split your group into four smaller sub-groups, each working on one of the areas. If you have a small group, maybe two groups can work on two headings each – just remember to give them more time to work. Another option is to ask your participants to 'gallery walk' the charts, writing in their responses on each chart.
4. Encourage the group to reflect on the 'so what?' of their analysis, having explored and reflected on the whole. For example, you could ask the group to consider the major impacts in each area, and what might this mean for the team and the organisation. Highlight these significant points on the charts using a contrasting marker pen.

Watch out!

In the event of asking participants to add their own individual points to the charts, request that they don't add identical points to others already given. If they agree with a response they could simply place a tick next to it to indicate agreement. That way space is available for new and different content.

Resources and kit

Flipchart, marker pens, tape and ruler/straight edge.

Catherine's expert insight

'What strikes me about this tool – both as a facilitator and from having been part of a group using the tool – is that it serves not only to gather useful data and content but also to grow team appreciation for the varied expertise and awareness that different members of the group bring to the conversation.

I think the secret of success here lies in encouraging people to state the patently obvious as well as more sophisticated or 'smart' observations. By using PEST to 'snapshot' where a situation or organisation is today it can mature a group's thinking into considering the current situation as part of a continuously developing story – rather than 'the truth' about how things are and always will be.

As well as asking for the obvious, a question such as "What might we be tempted to ignore?" or "What would we be crazy not to pay attention to?" can pay dividends by opening up conversation topics that until that point it has felt uncomfortable or inappropriate to raise.'

Political

Economic

WE ARE HERE

Social

Technological

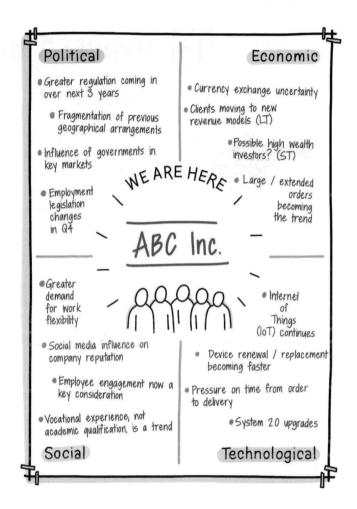

Political

- Greater regulation coming in over next 3 years
  - Fragmentation of previous geographical arrangements
- Influence of governments in key markets
- Employment legislation changes in Q4

Economic

- Currency exchange uncertainty
- Clients moving to new revenue models (LT)
- Possible high wealth investors? (ST)
- Large / extended orders becoming the trend

WE ARE HERE

ABC Inc.

Social

- Greater demand for work flexibility
- Social media influence on company reputation
  - Employee engagement now a key consideration
- Vocational experience, not academic qualification, is a trend

Technological

- Internet of Things (IoT) continues
- Device renewal / replacement becoming faster
- Pressure on time from order to delivery
  - System 2.0 upgrades

15 PROCESS MAP

Overview

Process mapping is not a new technique, nonetheless it remains a powerful method of growing understanding, especially when the subject at hand is complex with various interdependencies.

There's probably not much that goes on in organisations that cannot be explained as a process. Mapping a process can be hugely beneficial when you have a diverse range of brains in the room. Many processes involve people from a variety of functions, such as IT, marketing, production, sales and finance. All may have touchpoints with each other throughout a process.

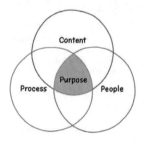

The Meeting Kaleidoscope

Don't be deceived by the name: this tool is designed to take detailed content and make it simple to understand for all involved.

Flow flavour

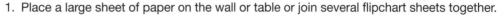

1. Place a large sheet of paper on the wall or table or join several flipchart sheets together.
2. Give your chart a title that reflects the process you are mapping, for example 'Intern Recruitment Process' or 'Supplier Invoicing Process'.
3. Provide participants with access to the markers and sticky notes and encourage them to start adding the stages of the process using the sticky notes. If your process has distinct phases you may wish to ask participants to focus on specific stages and work in parallel, joining up their thinking later. This will reduce the risk of duplication.
4. Encourage participants to be as specific as possible during the mapping process, for example by giving the step a title, brief description, purpose and listing who is involved.
5. Where groups are working in parallel and have concluded their thinking, invite the groups to join up the process end to end in order to see the whole. Review together.
6. When the process is agreed, draw lines onto the process in order to illustrate the flows and links.
7. Your process map is finished! To stretch the group's thinking why not invite others into the meeting who were not part of the mapping process in order to 'road test' the map with the group?

Watch out!

It can be easy to overlook an individual or function who has an impact on the process you are mapping. Make sure you have all functions represented in order to get the work done first time.

Resources and kit

Large sheet of paper, large sticky notes, marker pens, ruler/straight edge and tape.

Ben's expert insight

'Whether it's mapping a current process or the proposed future of a process, this methodology is a sure-fire way of getting to the bottom of its complexities.

Personally, I like to paper a wall or use multiple tables end to end so groups can huddle and visualise the "hotspots", challenges, blockages and inefficiencies. Naturally your group will also be able to see the ideas, innovations, resource savings and outcomes.

My big watch-out would be to decide beforehand what level of detail you intend to map the process to and then arm yourself with the right size and shape of material to make it a valuable business tool.'

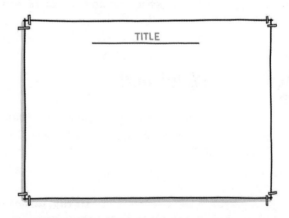

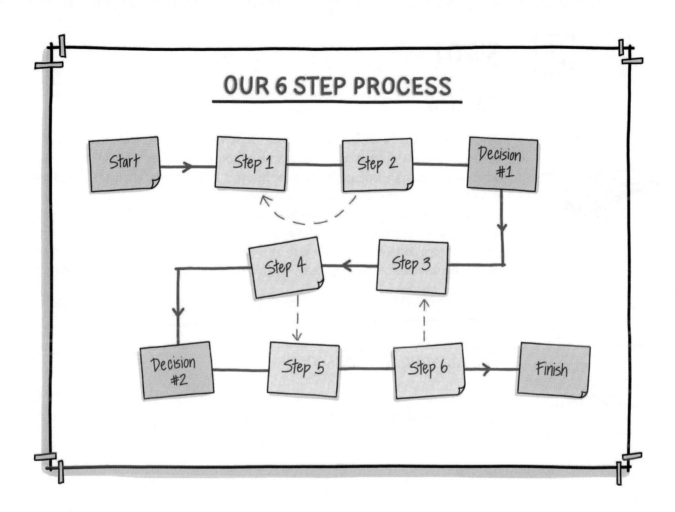

16 SWOT

Overview

SWOT, standing for Strengths, Weaknesses, Opportunities and Threats, is a commonly used and enduring business tool that enables the group to consider a current position using supportive and potentially obstructive factors. The tool can be used to analyse just about anything, from a product to a whole organisation or industrial sector.

It is generally accepted that strengths and opportunities are positive factors, and should be on one side of the grid, and weaknesses and threats, being countering elements, sit on the other side. Strengths and weaknesses tend to be regarded as 'internal' factors that are characteristic of the subject being explored (e.g., team, product), and opportunities and threats have an external bearing on the topic.

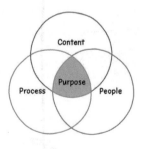

The Meeting Kaleidoscope

SWOT aims itself very much at content. Although some may prefer to approach SWOT in a specific order, the opportunity for everyone to contribute to all four areas is the key.

Flow flavour

1. Prepare a chart, preferably large, using a quadrant. A simple cross in the middle of the chart works well.
2. Add the titles, using the illustration as a guide. Ensure your main topic is clearly indicated.
3. As meeting leader you have a variety of choices as to how the group could work together. For example, you could ask each participant to add their comments to each quadrant, or split the group into two or four smaller groups.
4. Be clear on how you wish participants to add content to the chart, either by writing directly onto the chart or using sticky notes (one point per sticky note).
5. You also have a choice whether you wish groups to swap to review each other's input, or simply allow each group to share their thinking with the whole group.
6. Encourage the whole group to reflect on the 'so what?' of their analysis, having reflected on the whole. For example, you could ask the group 'What decisions might we make?' based on the SWOT, or even identifying several possible choices that could be considered using the Two by Two tool (Tool 29).

Watch out!

- Reminding the group about the internal and external differences (mentioned in the Overview above) will make for a more productive conversation.
- Everyone will have something valid to contribute. Ensure your process empowers everyone in the group to contribute their insights to each of the categories, either as the original starting group or when reviewing the work of others.

Resources and kit

A large sheet of paper (or four sheets of flipchart paper), marker pens, sticky notes, ruler/straight edge and tape.

Ben's expert insight

'This activity is indispensable. Whether you're working with a group to kick-start a project, review a team's progress, scope out a plan for next year or identify a new market, this tool offers a way of visually pooling everyone's different viewpoints.

For me the beauty in this simple activity is using it as a "giant notepad" to gather everyone's expert opinions on SWOT in one place. It gives all participants equal opportunity and space to add the insights they bring, from their very individual view of the work they must do together.

The chart then provides a snapshot of that moment in time and should be referred back to along the group's journey together.'

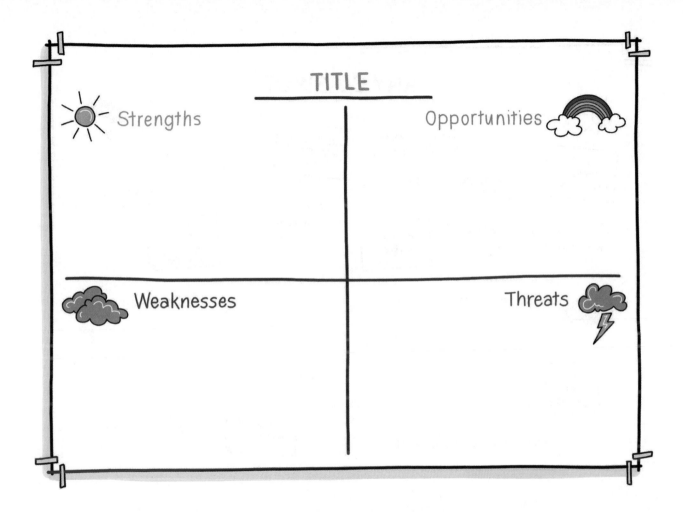

TITLE

Strengths

Opportunities

Weaknesses

Threats

ANY CO SWOT

Strengths

→ We can attract strong talent (for now)

Our systems are highly advanced

Our customer team has all FTE in place

• Our partner survey feedback is extremely strong

New Board in place

Opportunities

Growth of new tech channels to market

• More potential customers emerging as sector grows

Build on perceived role as sector influencer?

Emerging market diversification (time to cash)

Small competitors open to acquisition?

Weaknesses

→ We don't consistently maximise whole system capability

Our decision making can be slow

• We regularly enter into 'end of quarter panic'

Parent company decisions not always clear

Threats

→ Component costs are likely to increase

Competitor X has strong marketing strategy

Could we be acquired????

• Possible merger of competitor Y and Z

17 | TIMELINE

Overview

All organisations and teams have their history; however this history is often overlooked in meetings and considered a frivolous use of time compared to planning and working on future plans. Understanding why the team has got to where it is now provides a deep and rich source of insights, many of which can shape how the team works in the future.

The Timeline tool is very simple to create and use in a meeting. Use this tool before you start to consider the current reality, such as 'We are here' (Tool 14). It will give you a strong basis upon which to level the understanding within the team, especially when there is a mix of length of service in the team.

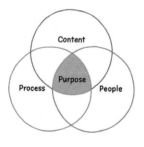

The Meeting Kaleidoscope

Content and People weave together here. People tend to like sharing their experiences and the Timeline allows them to do just that, within a broad content framework.

Flow flavour

1. Hang and create a chart, preferably as wide as possible, using the example illustration for inspiration. Along the bottom of the chart prepare a timeline. On the left-hand side start with a significant date, such as the date when the longest-serving member of the team started or when a project began, and on the right end with today.

2. Divide your timeline into three rows. The bottom row is for the team itself, the middle row is for the function in which the team operates, and the top row is for the organisation.

3. Ask your participants to plot when they joined the organisation on the timeline. This can be written onto the chart directly or added on a sticky note.

4. Task participants with writing key milestones directly onto the chart or using sticky notes. You might choose to split the group into three smaller groups, one group per row. Remember that everyone will need to input into all rows, so you may choose to give each smaller group an amount of time to focus on one row before rotating onto another.

5. Once everyone has contributed to the timeline, encourage the group to take a step back and review the chart as a whole. Ask participants questions to describe what they are noticing, the key learnings and Aha! moments, and what this all means for how this group takes the next step. Guide the group to look across the rows to spot linking themes and impacts.

Watch out!

It can be tempting for participants to fall into the trap of making judgements and applying their opinions rather than focussing on facts. Histories often include positive and negative memories; therefore your role is to acknowledge all memories and draw out details of relevant events.

Resources and kit

A large sheet of paper, marker pens (thin), sticky notes, ruler/straight edge and tape.

Helen's expert insight

'I can offer two insights here – both of which I learned early in my use of timelines:

1. At first, I underestimated how long a timeline session could take and planned a 45-minute slot. I misjudged how engaged the group would become in the exercise and we ended up taking 90 minutes which put the whole agenda timing out of whack. Since then I always plan in enough time so that the group can enjoy story-telling as they work through their history.

2. I was sometimes met with scepticism by team leaders who held a belief that there was no value in thinking about the past ("We need to think about the future!"). I was able to convince them of the value of learning from history in helping plan the future. When I see those leaders today, they usually remind me how the timeline session was one of *the most valuable* sessions they've ever done because it helped them see repeating patterns of strengths, weaknesses, behaviours, decision-points, blockers, enablers. This, in turn, helped them build future plans on strong foundations.'

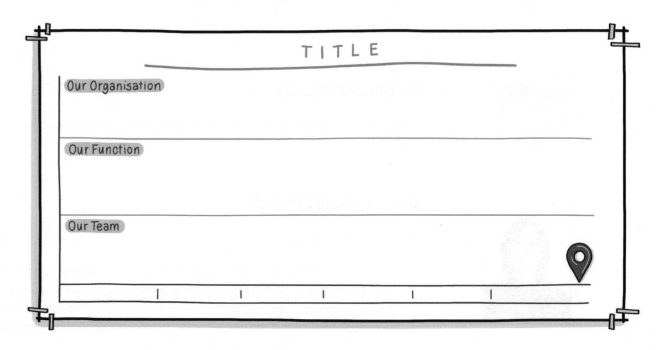

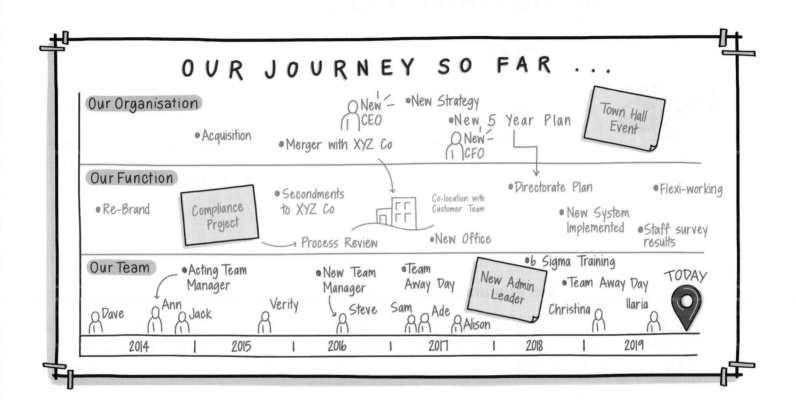

OUR JOURNEY SO FAR ...

Our Organisation

- Acquisition
- New CEO
- Merger with XYZ Co
- New Strategy
- New 5 Year Plan
- New CFO
- Town Hall Event

Our Function

- Re-Brand
- Compliance Project
- Secondments to XYZ Co
- Co-location with Customer Team
- Process Review
- New Office
- Directorate Plan
- New System Implemented
- Flexi-working
- Staff survey results

Our Team

- Acting Team Manager
- New Team Manager
- Team Away Day
- New Admin Leader
- 6 Sigma Training
- Team Away Day
- TODAY

Dave — Ann — Jack — Verity — Steve — Sam — Ade — Alison — Christina — Ilaria

| 2014 | 2015 | 2016 | 2017 | 2018 | 2019 |

18 INSPIRATION FILTER

Overview

Generating ideas is usually something human beings are perfectly capable of; however filtering all those ideas can be a tricky process, especially with so many views and opinions 'bumping' into each other.

The Inspiration Filter is designed to assist the filtering of generated ideas according to criteria that are important to the organisation. Like an actual hopper, ideas are placed in the top to be considered and evaluated (filtered). All ideas are welcome and carry equal value.

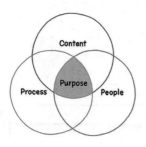

The Meeting Kaleidoscope

The ideas generated are the focal point, therefore this tool is focussed on Content. Having said that, the process is key here, particularly the integrity of the criteria used to pass ideas through the filter.

Flow flavour

1. Create your chart, as tall as possible, using the example illustration for inspiration. The headings you choose for the filter will need to be applicable to your organisation and context. Add the title to reflect the question or topic being explored.

2. Lead the group through the first stage to identify as many ideas as possible, responding to your question. Each idea should be written on one sticky note, which is then added to the hopper area at the top of the chart. Once all ideas have been provided it's time to start filtering.

3. Your first filter criteria should be applied to all the ideas in the hopper. Using the Knowledge Zone tool (Tool 12) could be especially helpful here when the group are making objective assessments. Each idea should be evaluated against that criteria and accepted or 'rejected'. Accepted ideas are passed down through into the next section in the filter. Rejected ideas are not lost, however, as they pass into a holding hopper for possible future consideration – called 'Not for Now' in the example.

4. The same process applies to the next level of filtering, applying the criteria to all ideas. Again, accepted ideas pass down the filter and rejected ideas pass to the holding hopper. You can add more criteria further down the filter if needed, especially if you have many ideas passing through.

5. The final filter process will lead to ideas that the group agree to take forward for deep exploration and/or implementation. If you still have a large number of ideas remaining, you may choose to use decision-making tools such as Visual Voting (Tool 30) or Show Me the Money! (Tool 31) to enable the group to decide which final ideas to progress, or alternatively you may choose someone to have the casting vote.

Watch out!

- This tool and process is likely to test your meeting leadership skills. The consideration of each idea at each stage of the filtering process needs to take place objectively and smoothly. The clarity of the filtering criteria is critical here, so that all participants fully understand how they are making their decisions using the evidence available. This is likely to be difficult for some participants, especially if they are particularly keen on their own ideas.
- You can use the PREP tool (Tool 2) at the start of the meeting to agree the ways of working, clearly explaining the need for everyone to be objective. Ask the group how they would like to work together to ensure complete objectivity.

Resources and kit

A large sheet of paper, marker pens, sticky notes, ruler/straight edge and tape.

Catherine's expert insight

'Though this tool and process are anything but a game in terms of their power and effectiveness, ensuring that the group undertaking it are crystal clear regarding "the rules of play" will be crucial to the smooth running of this session. As you work through it, it's worth remembering that rigorous debate is a sign that it is a conversation worth having!

Knowing what the group will do in the case of differing views/disagreement is crucial. It's also worth noting that the pace and physical output of the conversation are likely to be "lumpy". Expect flurries of thought and periods of silence. Please remember that silence is not a bad thing – sometimes you may be tempted to fill the gap. Watch out – be careful not to get in the way of fresh thoughts! Be confident and help the group to feel comfortable with periods of silence – give new thinking the time and space to develop.'

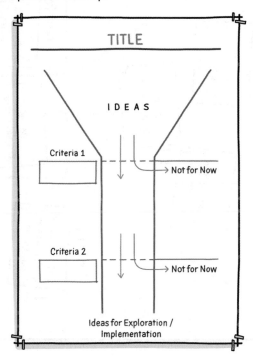

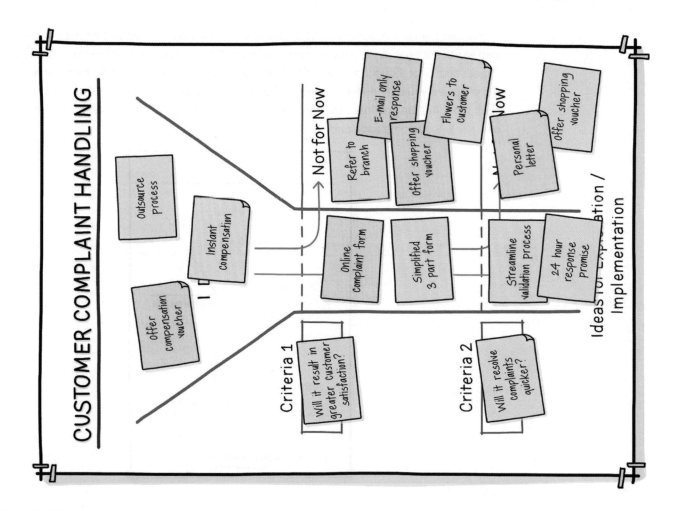

CUSTOMER COMPLAINT HANDLING

Outsource process

Instant Compensation

Offer compensation voucher

Not for Now

Refer to branch

E-mail only response

Offer shopping voucher

Flowers to customer

Now

Personal letter

Offer shopping voucher

Online Complaint form

Simplified 3 part form

Streamline validation process

24 hour response Promise

Ideas for Exploration / Implementation

Criteria 1
Will it result in greater customer satisfaction?

Criteria 2
Will it resolve complaints quicker?

19 GROW

Overview

GROW is a simple method used for problem solving and setting goals. The model was created by Sir John Whitmore and colleagues in the 1980s. It was popularised in Sir John's best-selling book, *Coaching for Performance*, and is extensively used during coaching. The four core components of the model are Goal, Reality, Options and Will.

In a meeting context GROW is an excellent tool to use when developing clear intent. Although it lacks the detail of the 'SWOT' and 'We are here' tools (in terms of a current reality assessment) it allows the group to springboard quickly and confidently into action whilst taking into account the current environmental position.

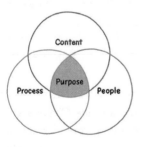

The Meeting Kaleidoscope

The precise order (or process) in which the content is captured in GROW is important. Ensure you work through in the correct order as it is difficult to truly know what options exist without setting a goal first.

Flow flavour

1. Prepare four charts, with the relevant title for each stage in the GROW process. You may wish to use a flipchart or large sheets of paper if you are working with a bigger group.

2. Start with the Goal stage. Your participants may already be clear on what the goal should be, but whether they are or not the priority is to be very clear on what the goal is in measurable terms. Use sticky notes to test thinking until the group has settled on the final, tangible goal. At that point remove the sticky notes and write the goal on the chart.

3. Move to the Reality stage. Ask participants to contribute to this section by providing observations about the current reality relevant to the topic. For example, if the goal is to reduce staff turnover from 8% to 5% in the next 12 months, the observations here may highlight what is currently affecting turnover. Allow the group some time to stand back and take in the whole picture.

4. Next comes the Options stage. The thinking will be about what could be possible based on the intended goal and the current reality. Encourage participants to let go of judgement and explore what could be. A good question here is 'If our success were completely guaranteed, what options might we explore?'

5. Before moving to the Will stage, allow more time for participants to think of other possible options. Don't be tempted to converge too early. Remember the 'groan zone' can be hugely helpful here, although it may not appear so to participants.

6. Finally, the Will stage is designed to identify what will be committed to based on the options generated in the previous stage. If you have used sticky notes in the Options stage the group may transfer relevant ideas to the Will chart, or edit if required. Your robust facilitation is important here in challenging whether these commitments are deliverable within the parameters set by the agreed goal.

Watch out!

- Being clear and specific really counts with this tool, especially at the Goal stage. If the goal of the group is, for example, to achieve more sales, this needs to be understood in measurable terms, such as how many sales to which customers, what percentage of growth and so on. The Knowledge Zone (Tool 12) could be hugely useful in supporting the group's thinking here.
- Be aware of judgement creeping in, especially at the Reality and Options stages. It may be tempting for participants to apply their opinions and views and you may need to help them in checking out the facts.
- Using a process that allows individual participants to contribute their own ideas, especially at the Options stage, will prevent any louder voices from inhibiting their ideas. Using sticky notes for all to silently capture ideas is a good option to have ready in this situation.
- When it comes to the Will stage, less is often more. Watch out for the group believing they can take on more than they can realistically deliver and question their thinking more deeply.

Resources and kit

Four large sheets of paper, large sticky notes, marker pens and tape.

Helen's expert insight

'I enjoy working with the GROW model to help a group. It provides a simple, over-arching framework for a meeting that helps teams and groups to be clear about where they are in the process. Beginning with a very clear Goal is most important to give a frame and focus for the discussions and decisions to come. In my experience, the more genuinely engaged the group are in defining Goal, Reality and Options, the greater the ease in reaching decisions and agreeing actions during Will.'

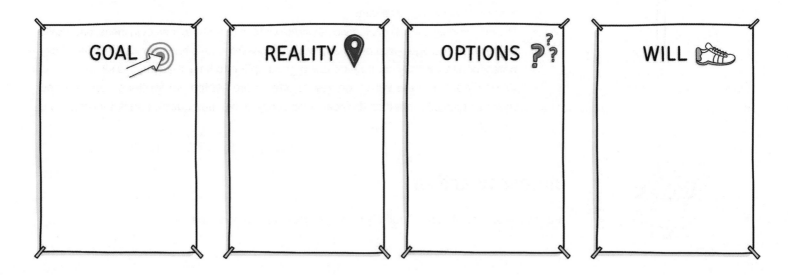

GOAL

Reduce staff turnover from 8% to 5% in the next 12 months

REALITY

- Staff turnover is higher in key departments, especially NPD

- Length of service in some areas is low

- We offer a median salary position in the market

- Our benefits package has been recently updated

OPTIONS ⁇

- Seek detailed feedback on why people are leaving
- Review salary positioning for key positions
- Review rewards and benefits package
- Check if trigger is a management style issue
- Measure take up of benefit usage
- Communicate what it's like to work here using employee testimonies

WILL

- Review the exit interview process to ensure quality of data

- Partner with managers in affected areas to provide support

- Review salary bandings for affected positions

- Review internal and external comms on benefits of working with us

[20] HUMAN CLUSTER

Overview

The purpose of the Human Cluster is to enable participants to discover where they might align (or not) on ideas and opinions based on the content being discussed. By its very nature it is an active process that many participants will find engaging, and provides an opportunity for participants to widen the number of people they work with. This tool will work best with larger groups of around 30+, and the visual resources needed are minimal.

Because there is no visual output per se for this process, such as a chart, you should use this tool as a way of grouping participants, potentially with an aim for those groups to explore and discuss their common idea. Depending upon the purpose and outcomes of your meeting you may wish to use another tool when the groups form.

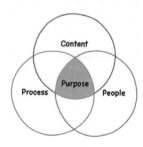

The Meeting Kaleidoscope

Here you will encounter an alignment of content with a distinctive personal flavour as participants interact and gather together to make sense of the information generated.

Flow flavour

1. Provide each participant with a sheet of paper and marker pen.
2. Ask participants to write, clearly and neatly, the response to the question you have posed. For example, 'What is the biggest opportunity we share?', or 'What challenge needs our attention right now?'
3. Invite participants to stand and clearly show their response so everyone can see it. Then ask participants to find other participants who have recorded either the same or a very similar response. Depending upon your group size this should usually take approximately 5 minutes.
4. The end result will be a number of groups formed by the alignment in their response to the question. Groups may be of varying sizes. If you have a particularly large group consider splitting into smaller groups to help the conversation flow whilst they still focus on the same topic.
5. Small groups also work; however if you have individuals who are not aligned to any group please ask them to join a group that they feel most closely reflects their view, and ask the group to ensure that this participant's view is taken into consideration within their conversation.

Watch out!

- The Human Cluster needs space in which to work. Make sure your participants can move easily and safely around the meeting space and remove all hazards.
- Remember to accommodate participants who may have special mobility needs.

Resources and kit

One sheet of plain paper or card (e.g., photocopying size) and a marker pen per participant.

Ben's expert insight

'The Human Cluster is a brilliantly quick way to inject some energy into a room, but I like to use it for other purposes too. You can use it as a way of prioritising or decision making, because for me the big insight is in the visual weighting of group sizes; this really demonstrates where the group's attention is.

As a meeting leader I will want to get more curious and understand the similarities, differences and juxtapositions between the sub-groups.

I also enjoy engagement and movement between the sub-groups as it increases understanding. So, as a fun build you could let the group know they'll have the chance to increase their group size! Ask each sub-group to share a 60-second "elevator speech" on why their group's topic is the right one to focus on. Then watch the changes and see where this leaves the group's commitment.'

STRETCHING

21 JOURNEY/TRANSITION MAP

Overview

The Journey/Transition Map is a sophisticated visual tool that can be used to deepen the group's collective thinking about where they have come from, where they are now and where they wish to head. The beauty of this tool is that, as the meeting leader, you have complete control over the level of sophistication of the image and what you are asking the group to consider. You could also adapt the image to suit the context in which you are working, or make it completely different.

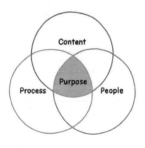

The Meeting Kaleidoscope

This is a tool with a deeper focus on Content, hence its place in the Stretching stage. At its best it is supported by a simple process and good facilitation questions.

Flow flavour

1. Prepare your chart using a simple image on which your key questions will be placed. There should be a link between the image you are using and the question you are posing. For example, dark clouds on a landscape image could represent difficult organisational conditions, or a pile of boxes might represent the resources a group needs.

2. Explain the chart to the group, including all the questions you have posed. For example, if your image flows from left to right, explain the chart using that flow.

3. Depending upon the size of your group you might wish to split the group into smaller (potentially mixed) sub-groups, each focussing on one or two questions. Be clear on the time they have been given to undertake this task (e.g., 20–30 minutes).

4. Ask the sub-groups to reflect on their questions, and to note their answers on sticky notes, one response per sticky note. These can be placed on the chart in the relevant area.

5. At this point you should have a chart populated with sticky notes. As a whole group, review the responses to each question so that all participants have sight of every answer. If there are any responses on which disagreement exists, focus on the underlying reasons and seek to converge on the point once all views are expressed. You should try to work at a steady pace here.

6. You might be working alongside a co-facilitator who can write the agreed responses directly onto the chart, thereby removing all the sticky notes. This is not essential, but it may help crystallise the points as you work through them.

7. By the end of this process you should have a fully populated journey map. Your group is now in a position to explore each area in more depth. For example, if you asked the group to identify the resources they need to reach their destination, they could now consider how they will obtain these resources and from whom. Likewise if they identified resistance from another department, how will they go about seeking to work with that department in order to allay their fears?

Watch out!

- Although this tool is essentially a drawing, it certainly doesn't need to be a masterpiece. A simple line drawing, with a little pastel for emphasis, will be perfectly sufficient.
- Avoid constructing an image that is too busy or sophisticated, as this could easily confuse the group.
- Go large! Use a big chart here – you will be glad of the space when the groups return with their insights.
- Ensure the image you are using will be acceptable and relevant to the group. The image is intended to serve the process, not distract from it.
- The questions you pose will be critical. Make time to carefully consider what you are asking *and* how the question is constructed to really stretch thinking.

Resources and kit

A large sheet of paper (as large as possible), marker pens, pastels, sticky notes, ruler/straight edge and tape.

Helen's expert insight

'Journey/Transition Maps are great to use when a group is at a point of change. In this case it helps to arrange the map into three sections, e.g.,

> OUR PAST – where we have come from/what got us here
> OUR PRESENT – our current reality/how we think and feel about our current situation
> OUR FUTURE – success for us would be. . . ?

To help the group to get started you could give an example in each area.

Don't be surprised if you find people telling stories about the past. This can be a good, cathartic experience for the group and can help to create a shared sense of history as well as bringing newcomers up to speed. Give the gift of time here.

You may find people a little more cautious when sharing how they feel about the current reality, especially if the change they are experiencing is not straightforward. Consider getting people to share thinking in "safe" pairs first before discussing as a group.

Imagining the future is helped by doing something to stimulate the group's thinking first, for example a walk outside, refreshment break or simply switching seats will bring a fresh perspective and bring about new energy.'

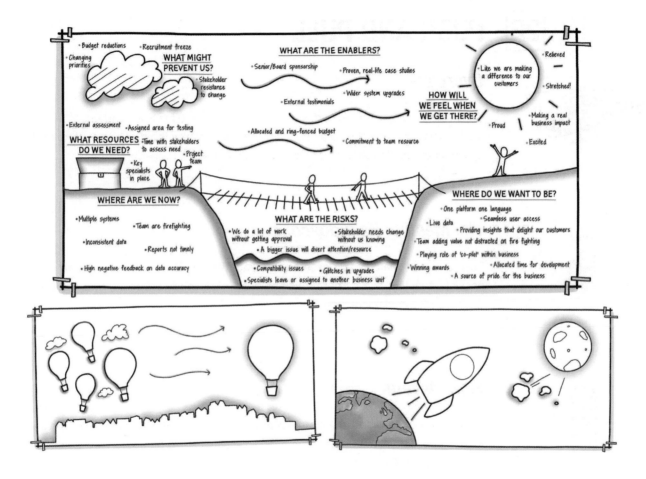

WHAT MIGHT PREVENT US?
- Budget reductions
- Recruitment freeze
- Changing priorities
- Stakeholder resistance to change

WHAT ARE THE ENABLERS?
- Senior/Board sponsorship
- Proven, real-life case studies
- External testimonials
- Wider system upgrades
- Allocated and ring-fenced budget
- Commitment to team resource

HOW WILL WE FEEL WHEN WE GET THERE?
- Like we are making a difference to our customers
- Relieved
- Stretched!
- Making a real business impact
- Proud
- Excited

WHAT RESOURCES DO WE NEED?
- External assessment
- Assigned area for testing
- Time with stakeholders to assess need
- Project team
- Key specialists in place

WHERE ARE WE NOW?
- Multiple systems
- Team are firefighting
- Inconsistent data
- Reports not timely
- High negative feedback on data accuracy

WHAT ARE THE RISKS?
- We do a lot of work without getting approval
- Stakeholder needs change without us knowing
- A bigger issue will divert attention/resource
- Compatibility issues
- Glitches in upgrades
- Specialists leave or assigned to another business unit

WHERE DO WE WANT TO BE?
- One platform one language
- Seamless user access
- Live data
- Providing insights that delight our customers
- Team adding value not distracted on fire fighting
- Playing role of 'co-pilot' within business
- Winning awards
- Allocated time for development
- A source of pride for the business

22 | PUSH AND PULL

Overview

If your need is to explore two sides of a given idea or topic the Push and Pull tool does the job. This tool's basic structure, akin to a forcefield analysis, enables the group to explore each perspective and work out the 'so what?' of their findings together.

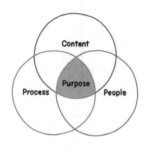

The Meeting Kaleidoscope

Push and Pull primarily focusses on content. The tool is hugely useful when identifying where possible enablers and barriers 'push against' each other, especially when applied to practical issues of idea implementation.

Flow flavour

1. Prepare a large chart with two arrows facing each other, using the example illustration for inspiration. Allow space in the middle between arrow tips. Add your idea, topic or question to be considered.

2. Your headings above each arrow should indicate counteracting forces, such as 'Enablers' and 'Barriers'. I recommend your right-facing arrow is your positive force, and the left-facing arrow is the 'negative' force.
3. Focus the group on the topic to be discussed. Depending upon the overall size of the group you may wish to split the group into two sub-groups, each focussing on a different arrow.
4. Allow the group time to discuss and explore, using sticky notes to record their contributions.
5. After approximately 20 minutes invite the groups to swap, and focus on the other perspective, building (but not removing) points added by the previous group.
6. Once complete lead the whole group in a conversation about their findings. It will be useful to match enablers and barriers together if they are focussed on the same point.
7. In the space between the arrows add a provocative question such as 'So what?', or 'What does this mean for us?', and ask the group to make sense of the whole by reflecting together on the key headlines. The group may gain benefit from asking whether any of the 'negative' forces are offset by the 'positive' forces.
8. Capture these summary insights yourself or ask the group to do that themselves.

Watch out!

Ensure you clearly frame the tool purpose to the whole group and allow the group to seek clarity if needed. This will help you to avoid very different approaches between groups.

Resources and kit

A large sheet of paper (preferable), marker pens (thin nib), sticky notes, ruler/straight edge and tape. If you don't have a lot of wall space use three flipchart sheets in landscape on a table.

Tom's expert insight

'I've used this tool many times in workshops focussed on business planning. I'm often intrigued by the speed with which the positive force (Enablers) is populated, especially when people are excited about a new idea or concept. It can take longer for potential barriers to be identified although there may be participants in your meeting who adopt a more realist approach and have no difficulty in describing what might get in the way. What's critically important to remember is that each perspective is equally valid, and it's the "So What?" ("what does this all mean?") that is critical to the group's thinking.'

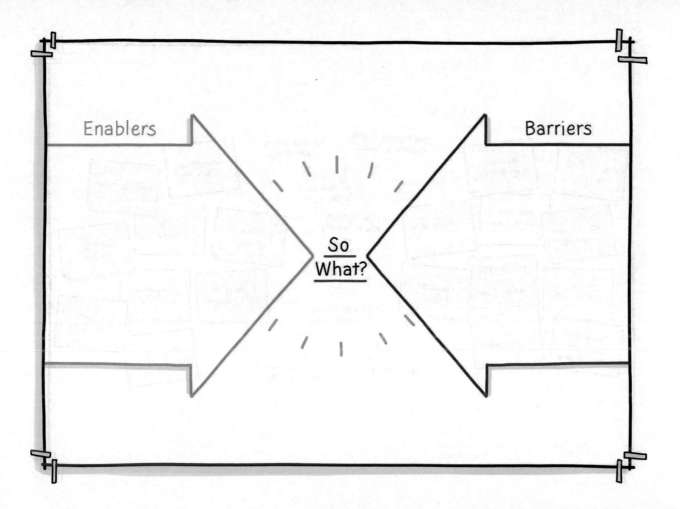

Enablers

Barriers

So
What?

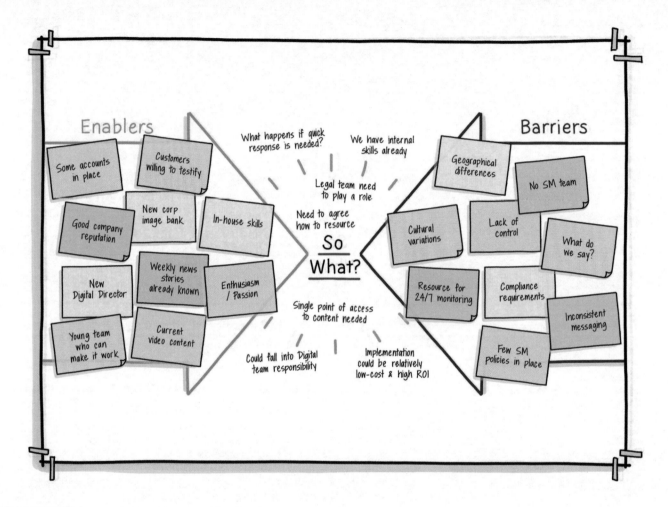

Enablers

- Some accounts in place
- Customers willing to testify
- Good company reputation
- New corp image bank
- In-house skills
- New Digital Director
- Weekly news stories already known
- Enthusiasm / Passion
- Young team who can make it work
- Current video content

So What?

- What happens if quick response is needed?
- We have internal skills already
- Legal team need to play a role
- Need to agree how to resource
- Single point of access to content needed
- Could fall into Digital team responsibility
- Implementation could be relatively low-cost & high ROI

Barriers

- Geographical differences
- No SM team
- Cultural variations
- Lack of control
- What do we say?
- Resource for 24/7 monitoring
- Compliance requirements
- Inconsistent messaging
- Few SM policies in place

23 'THERE IS NEVER ANY MILK!'

Overview

You might be wondering why on earth this tool is called 'There is never any milk!' The truth is that I could have used many statements here but I chose this abstract example so you are more likely to remember it later when you are choosing your tools.

This is a tool about reframing a statement into a question that will allow the group to identify the action needed to move them forward, particularly if they happen to be 'stuck' in thinking that focusses on the problems they are experiencing rather than the solutions needed to make progress. The alternative question to this statement might be 'How can we ensure there is always enough milk?' In a business context a common statement might be 'We never seem to get agreement on the budget', whereas the positive questioning alternative might be 'What will it take to reach agreement on the finance needed?'

This tool doesn't necessarily need to be pre-planned, although you may hear some of the statements in your preparation before the meeting. If you do hear statements that might benefit from being transformed into a question, make a note of them and keep them safe in case you need to refer to them later.

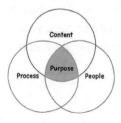

The Meeting Kaleidoscope

Whilst content is important, it is the process used to move from statement to question that 'unlocks' the door to insights that move the group forward.

Flow flavour

1. Select the statements that appear to be most commonly used in your meeting. There may be one or two that stand out, or you may hear several. If you hear a number of statements reflect them back to the group and check which statements they would most like to focus on (e.g., those that are likely to have most impact if they are addressed). The group might choose to vote (Tool 30) if there are many to choose from.
2. Invite the group to identify a positive question that can be used to explore the issue(s). You could use the title of this tool (and its question alternative) to illustrate the purpose of the process itself.
3. As the group identifies the positive questions, note these as headings on several flipchart sheets. These might already be arranged on the wall around the room for speed.
4. Once all the statements have been transformed into questions invite the group to review each question and note their responses directly onto the flipchart.
5. Depending upon the size of the group you might ask them to split into smaller groups to work on a question, or you could invite everyone individually to respond by walking around the charts and adding their insights.
6. Review the responses together, especially if participants have worked on different charts, as they may wish to add their contributions to the questions they have not worked on.
7. Seek agreement on the actions that could be taken to really make progress. You might consider using a voting process (Tool 30) if you have a variety of suggestions. Those suggestions that are most popular might form the focus that your group takes next.

Watch out!

The questions the group suggests might be powerful and can be used immediately. It might be possible that a suggested question needs a little more refinement. Be careful not to provide the group with your suggested alternative, and instead ask how the question might be improved in the relevant area.

Resources and kit

Several sheets of flipchart paper, marker pens and tape.

Catherine's expert insight

'I love this tool. It reveals the power of language so neatly. By changing the angle from which an issue is explored to one of curiosity rather than complaint the world becomes a different place! Change the words and you change the mindset. A group can move from "stuck" to brimming with ideas in moments. Use it!'

STATEMENTS

1. We never have the time to really understands each others needs

2. Our systems are too slow to keep up with order demand

3. It's hard to find the right people to work in our business

---

1. We never have the time to really understands each others needs

---

2. Our systems are too slow to keep up with order demand

---

3. It's hard to find the right people to work in our business

STATEMENTS

1. We never have the time to really understands each others needs

2. Our systems are too slow to keep up with order demand

3. It's hard to find the right people to work in our business

---

1. We never have the time to really understands each others needs

- More focussed time in our meetings about how we are working
- I:Is with each other on a regular basis
- A day shadowing each other
- A team away day
- Commit to an hour per week simply focussed on us
- Try 30 degree feedback??

---

2. Our systems are too slow to keep up with order demand

- Remove first checking step in order system
- Review what information we actually need
- Review supplier base and filter out slower partners
- Shorten lead times on smaller orders through a partner delivery contract

---

3. It's hard to find the right people to work in our business

- Focus more heavily on university population
- Strengthen our apprenticeship offer
- Publicise benefits at an early stage in the recruitment process
- Take part in a great place to work survey
- Enhance our presence at recruitment fairs

24 PICTURE CARDS

Overview

Images are incredibly powerful tools for drawing out thoughts, feelings and emotions, and this applies within the meeting environment too. Pictures on their own will go some way to eliciting a response from your participants; however it is the question you pose to the group when using the images that will give you powerful conversations to work with.

You don't need to purchase an expensive custom-made deck of images, although this will certainly save you time. Consider using postcards, or even taking photographs yourself that can be printed and used in a deck.

The process below is a suggested approach to using this tool. Of course you can choose whatever question you wish depending upon the circumstances, and you can introduce this tool in other stages of the meeting, such as Opening, Working and Moving.

The Meeting Kaleidoscope

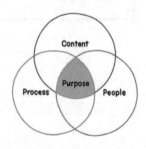

I like this tool for the insights it consistently offers people in the meeting. Although your question may be intended to stretch thinking on content, it is how participants make the visual link between the image and the question that provides powerful information about how and what people are thinking.

Flow flavour

1. Spread your deck of images on the floor or a table, image facing upwards, so everyone in the group can see them. This often works well when the group is standing and formed in a circle around the cards.
2. Focus the group on the cards, and encourage them to look at the images for up to a minute without picking them up.
3. Explain that you will be posing a question to the group, and it is their task to pick an image that best conveys their response to the question.
4. Clearly pose the question to the group. For example: 'What might we be missing that needs our attention?' Repeat the question so that everyone has heard and understood it.
5. Invite the participants to choose their card, being mindful of others around them, and once they have picked their card to return to the place they were standing, with the card clearly visible to everyone.
6. Once everyone has chosen an image, invite someone to start by briefly explaining the image they have chosen, and their reasons for selecting it.
7. Repeat this process until everyone has explained their image.
8. Thank the group, summarise the exercise and explain the transition to the next part of the meeting.

Watch out!

- If you intend to create your own deck of picture cards ensure that you have selected a wide range of images that will appeal to your group.
- Choose images that are generic in nature, as this will increase the probability of the images resonating with a wider range of participants.
- Be very careful not to choose images that may offend, and respect any copyright restrictions on the images you use.

Resources and kit

A range of approximately 50–60 pictures, such as postcards or photographs, ideally no smaller than playing-card size.

Ben's expert insight

'If you are going to invest in any piece of kit after the basics, this would be my recommendation. These photo cards are so valuable to have available in meetings. Here's why in my eyes.

Speed – they help groups access their perspectives super-quickly and can save much time in meetings.

Simplicity – the cards are a way of helping participants sift through huge amounts of data and prioritise their many comments into one image.

Equality – you are guaranteed to hear from every person without pressurising anyone and we appreciate that is not always easy.

But the power is in the wrap-up conversation. What were the insights? Differences? Similarities? And what now. . . ? Ensure this conversation ends in value, whether it is increased understanding, prioritisation of topics, identification of next steps.'

25 | ENHANCED IDEA

Overview

The Enhanced Idea tool uses a simple methodology to swiftly analyse an idea and, potentially, make it even better. The tool isn't limited to ideas and concepts either, as it can be used on just about anything, including processes.

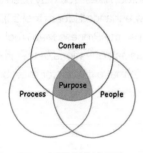

The Meeting Kaleidoscope

Both Content and Process are important in order to reach the new, enhanced idea. Process is really important, however, or the conversation could simply wander.

Flow flavour

1. Prepare your chart, divided into four columns, using the headings provided in the example illustration.
2. Add your group's ideas, which may have arisen from the Working stage of the meeting to the far-left column so they can be easily seen.

3. Invite your group to consider each idea (you may wish to split the group into smaller groups), first considering what works in column 2 and then what doesn't work in column 3. It may be advisable to introduce criteria against which the idea can be assessed. For example: 'Does the idea lead to a reduction in administration?' Using sticky notes for responses will allow participants to adapt their thinking as they go.

4. Finally, the group proposes an idea that is an enhanced version of the idea presented in column 1.

5. Encourage participants to share the enhanced ideas with each other and invite comment to build upon their thinking.

6. Success! Your process has resulted in enhanced ideas that the group likes. You may need to ask participants to vote on their preferred idea if you have many new enhanced ideas (Tool 30). They can continue to work on the shortlisted ideas using a tool such as the Process Map (Tool 15).

7. If the group has not reached consensus on the enhanced ideas ask questions of the group to understand where objections lie, such as 'What would it take to make it work for everybody?' and continue to refine.

Watch out!

- Be careful to assume that an idea analysed using this tool will automatically result in an enhanced idea. The original idea might be astounding, in which case if it cannot be improved that is a great result in itself.

- Be mindful of personal opinion creeping in, especially when considering what doesn't work about an idea. As mentioned above, using criteria against which to consider the idea should provide for a consistent assessment, and will show up personal biases if they arise.

Resources and kit

A large sheet of paper, marker pens, sticky notes, ruler/straight edge and tape.

Helen's expert insight

'It is natural for personal bias to creep in during this process, especially by the originators (and their friends) of the ideas. One way to overcome this is first to acknowledge this as a possibility and then request that everyone takes an objective stance. This is a simple move, but I often find it is enough to get the whole group to work objectively.

If personal bias still exists, you can ask people to work on only the ideas they did not contribute.'

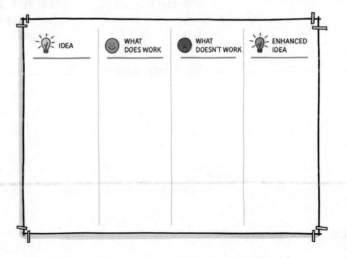

IDEA	WHAT DOES WORK	WHAT DOESN'T WORK	ENHANCED IDEA
→ Invite customers to view our new manufacturing line anytime in Q1	→ Strengthens client relationship → Enhances client understanding of our processes → Possible motivator for line staff → Easy to do → No / little cost	→ We cannot plan for an issue on the line → Not all line staff might wish or be able to do it → Having customers all together at the same time might be sensitive	→ A planned line show around for top 5 customers on specific dates in Q1 → A dedicated and briefed 'hospitality' team, recognised for their contribution

26 | DIFFERENT PERSPECTIVES

Overview

You will recall that in Section 3 we briefly explored the concept of the intersection, and how a range of perspectives in the conversation can lead to breakthrough ideas and innovation. The Different Perspectives tool can be particularly powerful if your participant group is as diverse as it can possibly be. Inevitably it may not always be possible to have everyone you would like in the room, and you may need to use your best brains in the room to reflect on the view others might have expressed had they been right there with you.

This tool assumes that your group has an idea they wish to test with stakeholders who may have an influence upon its success. For example, this idea might have resulted from the use of the Enhanced Idea tool (Tool 25).

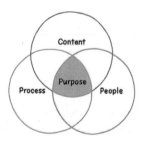

The Meeting Kaleidoscope

As the name suggests the Different Perspectives tool is focussed on people (stakeholders), although the content generated is the primary output.

Flow flavour

1. Ensure that all participants clearly understand the idea or proposal that is being considered.
2. Prepare your charts with the name of a stakeholder at the top of each chart, plus a small icon or photo if appropriate. A suggestion is to consider no more than three or four, and focus on those stakeholders who may have the most influence over progress made after the meeting. Ensure that all participants understand who each stakeholder is.
3. Divide the group into sub-groups, inviting them to work on a different stakeholder for a set period, for example 10–15 minutes. See the note below about adding further structure to the chart for consistency of response from the group.
4. After this period has concluded invite participants to move to another stakeholder chart. If they agree with points previously offered simply ask participants to add a tick next to the relevant point, or build upon it if they have something further to add.
5. When all participants have considered each stakeholder invite the whole group to share what this means to them, especially in terms of the actions they may need to take following the meeting. The Actions and Next Steps tool (Tool 35) might be a good way of capturing what needs to be done.

Watch out!

- Assumptions will no doubt be made about stakeholder perspectives. Use the whole group to check perceptions of potential reactions and try not to rely on the opinions of one or two people in the room, which could be a threat to your thinking.

- To add further structure you may wish to consider what each stakeholder would think, feel and do as a result of the idea being proposed (see example illustration). This will enhance consistency in the group's approach.

Resources and kit

A large sheet of paper, marker pens, sticky notes and tape.

Helen's expert insight

'I find it very helpful to add a photograph of the stakeholder to the chart. There is something about the group being able to see an individual's face that helps them imagine their perspective more deeply.

When using the Different Perspectives tool, it will serve you and the group well to introduce the process at the start of the meeting. In this way you will plant a seed in the minds of your group that they will be considering diverse perspectives from stakeholders who are not in the meeting. This will immediately stimulate thinking and discussion which will help contribution later.

You could consider having this tool available throughout the meeting (rather than at a set point). In this way, it can be contributed to at any point as on ongoing, parallel process and then reviewed later in the agenda.'

27 IN OUR DREAMS

Overview

Many groups find it hard to break out of present-day business constraints when they endeavour to imagine the future. This runs the risk of the group's thinking becoming pedestrian and 'same old, same old'. The In Our Dreams tool can be used when you seek fresh thinking without the constraints of today's practical needs. Its approach is based upon the belief that it is far more effective to create a compelling target to aim for and then map a clear path to that future target than to attempt to build a step-by-step plan from today towards an uninspiring target.

The Meeting Kaleidoscope

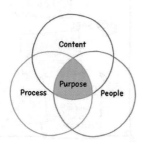

This tool creates the space to generate first-class content and to unite a group in creating something that they feel passionate about and are thus likely to support in making happen.

Flow flavour

1. Hang a large sheet of paper (big thinking is supported by big space!) and draw a cloud in the middle. Everybody who is working on this session needs to be able to see the whole piece of paper.

2. In the cloud write a positive statement, dated for an agreed point in the future, written in the present tense. For example: 'It's 1 November 2023 and we have achieved a 200% increase in visitor numbers. What have we done to get us here?'

3. Explain that you will be creating many options as a group and then vote for the ideas that should be explored further.

4. Make it clear that this is a chance to dream, to imagine having overcome barriers and constraints and to be able to do whatever it takes to reach the statement in the cloud.

5. Introduce the ways of working for the session, which are that all points are valid, difference is expected and valued and that the person speaking will tell the person writing where they want their idea to be shown.

6. Let the group know that it's time to start by introducing the date and their massive success! Something like... 'So here we are in 2023 – who would have believed we could achieve a 200% increase in visitor numbers? Let's take a look back at what we did.'

7. Write down the first idea that comes – and then follow the ways of working from there on until you have a rich set of options from which to pick. (See Tool 13 for advice on how to create Mind Maps.)

8. Help the group to stay 'in the future looking back' by saying things like 'I know there have been massive challenges over the last X years – what was your secret in overcoming them?' and 'What are you most proud of having done or not done?'

Watch out!

The group may feel a little self-conscious at speaking as if they are in the future looking back. Be definite about it and keep your language that of looking backwards until the group feel comfortable with it too – it doesn't take long! If you 'give in' and start looking forwards rather than looking back be aware that today's constraints and narrower thinking will be the result.

Resources and kit

A large sheet of paper (or, if you have to work smaller, scale down), marker pens and tape.

Catherine's expert insight

'Two things – the first is, if you can, ask someone else to record the group's work so that you can focus purely on leading the conversation.

The second? I'd reiterate the point above about holding your nerve until the group are confidently speaking as if it's the future date written in the bubble. This session requires some skill on your part to engage people in creating something that they really care about and their response will be massively influenced by your enthusiasm and language. By saying things like "We've achieved more than we dreamed possible – how have we made that happen?" and exuding genuine curiosity to know the details of how the group have worked and acted that have led them to massive success, you can create new pathways of thinking that will then be solidified from dreams into hard-hitting reality.'

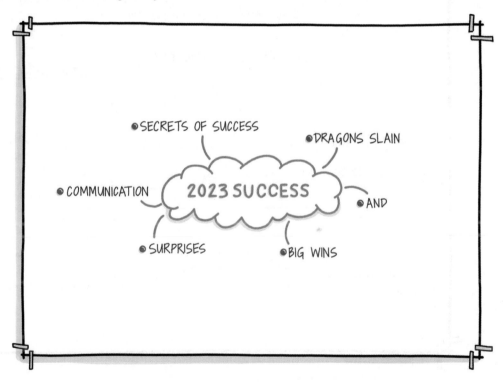

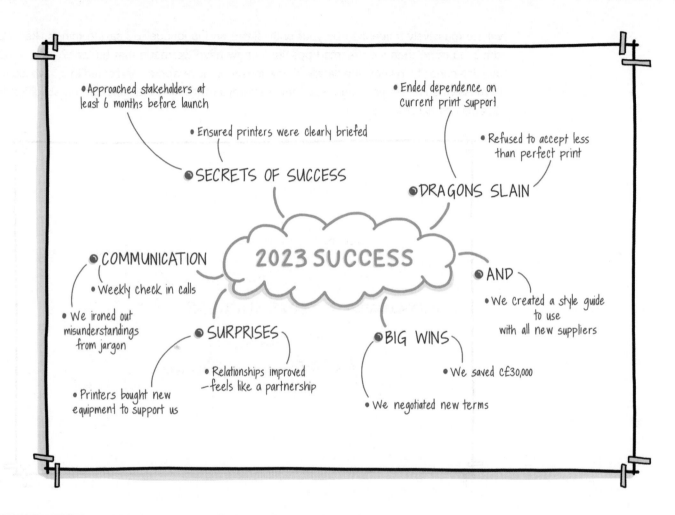

- Approached stakeholders at least 6 months before launch
- Ensured printers were clearly briefed

SECRETS OF SUCCESS

- Ended dependence on current print support
- Refused to accept less than perfect print

DRAGONS SLAIN

2023 SUCCESS

COMMUNICATION
- Weekly check in calls
- We ironed out misunderstandings from jargon

AND
- We created a style guide to use with all new suppliers

SURPRISES
- Relationships improved — feels like a partnership
- Printers bought new equipment to support us

BIG WINS
- We saved c£30,000
- We negotiated new terms

28 WHY? WHY? WHY? WHY? WHY?

Overview

If you've had a conversation with a child who asks why every time you say something you will know that this inquisitive approach can be fairly tiring. What we might be missing is that this is really an inspired approach to stretching thinking and deepening understanding.

Sometimes known as the '5 Whys', this is an approach designed to understand cause and effect relationships that might underlie a specific problem or scenario. The tool can also be used to understand reasons for taking a particular action. Every answer given provides the basis for the next question. You don't have to use five questions, as fewer questions may be appropriate. As a guide, try not to use more than seven.

I always think of Kaner's 'groan zone' when I use this tool, as participants often find it difficult to keep going but find the insights generated to be hugely useful.

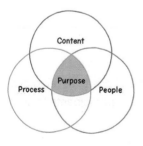

The Meeting Kaleidoscope

Content and Process are working together with this tool to bring about new thinking and insights.

Flow flavour

1. Prepare a simple chart with the issue or statement at the top, followed by 5 Whys underneath, each with enough spacing between them to capture responses. You may have several statements to analyse, in which case create as many charts as you need.
2. Invite participants to consider the statement, for example 'We need to streamline our customer feedback process', then ask them to respond to the first 'Why?'
3. Allow the group a short period of time to consider their response and ask them to write the answer on the chart. Try to avoid long conversations, as 10 minutes will be ample.
4. Once the first 'Why?' has been answered, participants should move to the next 'Why?' and repeat the process until all questions have been answered.
5. It is possible that a group may generate a new breakthrough insight after two or three questions. In this case avoid forcing them to continue with further questions if it would be a more valuable use of time to focus on the new thinking.
6. Use your questioning skills to explore what new or different thinking the process has uncovered. Does this change the group's thinking on the original topic? If so, what change of direction might be needed here?

Watch out!

- As mentioned above, participants may find this process difficult due to its repetitive nature. They will be in the 'groan zone' – hooray! Positively encourage participants to continue as much as you can.
- Personal opinions might creep in here, and could lead to disagreement. Make sure all voices are heard.

Resources and kit

Several sheets of flipchart paper, marker pens and tape.

Ben's expert insight

'Einstein reportedly said that if he only had one hour to solve a problem, he would spend 55 minutes defining the problem and the remaining 5 minutes solving it – this is the mindset within which this tool is most useful.

Analysing the root of a problem, barrier or opportunity is huge as it helps full group understanding and aligns the solution-generation element of the conversation with laser-like accuracy.

Just be aware that it can get a little dense in terms of data/material – managing that visually and flexibly is critical to a group perspective.'

TITLE

Why?

Why?

Why?

Why?

Why?

WE NEED TO DOUBLE THE QUANTITY OF END-USER FOCUS GROUPS

Why?

So we can obtain a broader set of detailed and constructive feedback data

Why?

To provide product team with relevant and accurate information

Why?

We must create an overall offer that users will fully engage with

Why?

Because we know they are not using all the product features

Why?

They might not know these exist, or are not telling us why.

DECIDING

29 TWO BY TWO

Overview

The Two by Two grid is a commonly used tool and is often known as The Boston Matrix, referring to the Boston Consulting Group who developed the tool in the 1970s. The grid is most commonly used when comparing ideas or activities.

   This tool is a simple yet powerful method of comparing options and testing assumptions. Categories such as urgency and impact, or cost and risk are often chosen for the axes. You can use the grid with whatever criteria you choose although the core assumption is that there will be a quadrant of the grid that is most favourable (e.g., low risk and low cost) and a quadrant that will be least favourable (e.g., high risk and high cost).

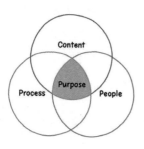

The Meeting Kaleidoscope

Content and Process are intersecting here, which is why the grid works well as a pragmatic method of making judgements using a simple tool.

Flow flavour

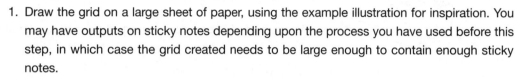

1. Draw the grid on a large sheet of paper, using the example illustration for inspiration. You may have outputs on sticky notes depending upon the process you have used before this step, in which case the grid created needs to be large enough to contain enough sticky notes.
2. Apply the criteria you will be working with to the bottom and left side of the grid, as shown in the illustration. Also indicate the extremes of high and low.
3. Guide your participants to decide where an idea (on a sticky note) might be placed on the grid, depending upon the perceived position on both axes.
4. Once complete, encourage the group to share their thinking with each other and, if appropriate, revise their judgement based on their conversation, before drawing out the key insights from the group.

Watch out!

It can be tempting for participants to get into detail about exactly where an idea should be placed on the grid. It is often beneficial to keep time short, so that participants are working using their gut instinct rather than overthinking.

Resources and kit

A large sheet of paper, marker pens, sticky notes, ruler/straight edge and tape.

Helen's expert insight

'A Two by Two grid can quickly become flooded with post-it notes if the group does not consolidate and align thinking first. It is natural to assume that adding everybody's ideas to the grid on sticky notes is an inclusive thing to do, but more often than not it just leads to confusion and frustration.

The key is to consolidate thinking and check the group's understanding of each idea *before* adding to the grid. Doing this will result not only in fewer post-it notes, but (more importantly) greater understanding between people. It is worth taking time to do this because it becomes a pre-decision step that will result in faster alignment and clarity when adding to the grid itself.

Finally, I know it is tempting for groups to waiver in their decision about which quadrant to place an idea in. They will often opt to place a post-it on the dividing line between quadrants rather than be definite about which section the idea should be placed in. In this case, ideas are literally placed "on the fence" and this can make final decision making less impactful.

Here, sticky notes come into their own because of their temporary nature. When all sticky notes have been added, encourage the group to move any "on the fence" ideas to the quadrant they should be in when compared to the other ideas on the grid. In this way, the final decisions will be bolder and clearer.'

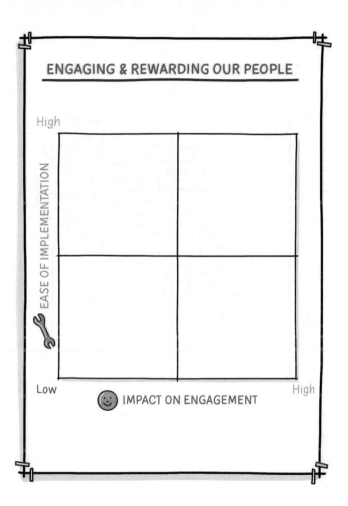

ENGAGING & REWARDING OUR PEOPLE

High

EASE OF IMPLEMENTATION

Low

IMPACT ON ENGAGEMENT

High

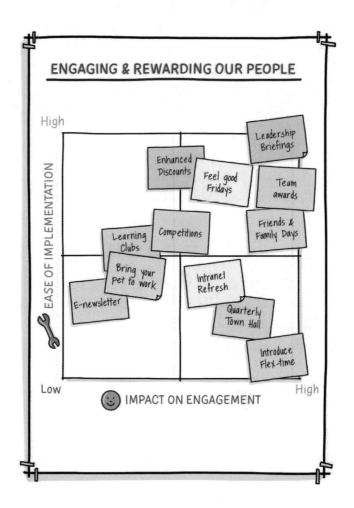

ENGAGING & REWARDING OUR PEOPLE

30 VISUAL VOTING

Overview

Democracy is a great thing, and meetings are places where democratic processes can shine. Visual Voting is a simple process of empowering participants to express their preferences openly in service of making collective decisions.

Usually this tool will be used once the group has generated a range of ideas, such as for a new product, strategy or action, with voting used to invite participants to select which concept they like best or would prefer to work on.

How many votes participants are given is purely up to you as the meeting leader. This largely depends on how many suggestions are made and how many participants you have in your meeting. As a general rule I suggest three votes per participant.

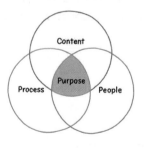

The Meeting Kaleidoscope

Visual Voting is grounded in fairness and democracy, so the process needs to be clear and fair for all to see.

Flow flavour

1. Once you have concluded on a range of ideas or proposals to be voted on, ensure that everyone is clear on what each idea means. Give all participants the opportunity to ask questions for clarification so they know exactly what they are voting for.
2. Provide each participant with a marker pen or voting dots if you have not already provided these.
3. Explain that you will be asking everyone to apply their votes and, critically, outline the criteria they should use when voting. For example, are you asking them to vote for the next product idea to be launched within 12 months, or on the idea that will have the biggest financial impact on the organisation?
4. Invite participants to vote, and to use all their allocated votes. This may take a little time depending upon the size of your group. Allow time for participants to carefully consider how they will vote.
5. Once all votes have been cast, add up the number of votes for each idea and add the total. This will allow participants to quickly see the final scores.
6. Summarise the outcome of the vote, orientating the group to the highest scoring concepts.
7. If you have clearly achieved the outcome, for example to decide on the top three workable ideas, you can move on to your next stage of the process. In the event of an inconclusive result, such as a tie, you may wish to award a casting vote to a specific individual who may or may not be in the meeting.

Watch out!

- Visual Voting is intended to give all participants the freedom to express their own opinions. You may wish to run this process silently if there is a chance that some participants may influence others in making their decision.

- Be clear about where and how participants can vote. For example, are you allowing them to apply their votes absolutely anywhere, which may include placing all their vote opportunities on one idea?
- Ensure there is physical space between the options that can be chosen. If information is placed too close together it can be difficult to know how many votes an idea has attracted.
- For complete transparency, if you are to allow a casting vote in the event of a tie, ensure participants are aware of this before the voting begins.

Resources and kit

Sticky dots (cut into strips for the appropriate number of votes) or marker pens.

Ben's expert insight

'A reliable tool, Visual Voting is still an under-used method for sifting and converging towards a powerful outcome. In my experience it can be used in any number of different moments. Here are some of my favourite examples.

- A tired meeting room – if it's been a long meeting and you can feel the energy draining, Visual Voting can often re-energise a group. So, use this to help them see light at the end of the tunnel.
- Participants who won't let go – sometimes people will not compromise and this needs to happen in teams. Visual Voting will show which ideas need to be compromised and left behind. Equally, which ones you can pick up and run faster with.'

Implement new customer
feedback process

Backdate client
performance report

Phase out
manual data upload

Upgrade product
testing facility

Create revised
web brochure

Move newsletter from
weekly to monthly

31 SHOW ME THE MONEY!

Overview

Show Me the Money! is a similar tool to Visual Voting, but with a fun twist. We were first alerted to this method when we each presented our own business ideas to a trusted advisor, who produced a bag of chocolate coins and allocated the coins to us based on his judgement about their likely success and profitability. Although a simple gesture, it was nonetheless powerful and I still have the coins on my desk in full view, as a sign of his trust in our thinking.

Don't worry if you cannot obtain chocolate coins, as you can use other items such as children's play money or other sweets. The point here is that the items are a visual symbol of trust and faith in an idea or concept.

Another advantage of this process is that you can invite others, who might not have been in the meeting, to come in and allocate their items. You will need to ensure that they fully understand each idea before you ask them to vote.

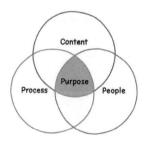

The Meeting Kaleidoscope

Show Me the Money! should, like Visual Voting, be a transparent process, and the way in which the process is undertaken will be key.

Flow flavour

1. To use this tool you should be at a stage where you have at least several ideas, concepts or proposals that have been identified as potentially viable for implementation, but a decision needs to be made about which of these ideas should receive the greatest energy.
2. Ensure all the ideas are clearly visible and well-spaced on a new, large sheet of paper, especially if the ideas are mixed in with other ideas from your previous process. This chart is best placed on a table rather than a wall, which means that the coins can be placed around the idea without needing to affix the items to the wall.
3. Allocate the coins, money or whatever items you are using to all participants.
4. Clarify the criteria which will be used by all participants when allocating their items. Writing the criteria on a flipchart is recommended so everyone can see them at any time in the process.
5. Invite participants to allocate their items. If you have limited physical space in the room, ensure that any chairs and bags are moved away from the voting area for safety.
6. Once all items have been allocated, encourage the group to stand back and review the scene. It might be obvious which items have received the most, but, if not, ask participants to count the items and, using a marker, write the amount next to the items on the chart.
7. You should now have an order of preference for implementation, and the group can start working on the all-important detail.

Watch out!

- Be clear about where and how participants can vote. For example, are you allowing them to allocate their items absolutely anywhere, which may include placing all their vote opportunities on one idea?
- For complete transparency, if you are to allow a casting vote in the event of a tie, ensure participants are aware of this before the voting begins.

Resources and kit

A table, a large sheet of paper, your voting items (chocolate coins, play money etc.), marker pens and tape.

Helen's expert insight

'In any process where voting is involved, there is a risk of peer pressure or "group think". For example, in a hierarchical organisation, people might assess how the boss might vote and then lean that way themselves to avoid being singled out. Or, if the group comprises peers (without a clear hierarchy), it could be that the dominant, vocal group members are persuasive enough to sway the vote throughout the group.

If either of these is a concern, you can use the following process to get around it:

- **Firstly**, explain that the opportunity to vote has arrived.
- **Then**, allow a few minutes of quiet personal reflection so that each person can order their thoughts and decide where their vote should be placed.
- **Next**, get everybody to move to place their vote at the same time without looking at the movement of others.

When all votes have been cast, get the group to stand back and observe and discuss what they see. The fun element of chocolate coins or paper money has the bonus of making the discussion that follows feel light-hearted and encourages an atmosphere of "serious play" that quite often helps to set a positive tone for the group to share differences in thinking.'

32 | WE WILL, WE MIGHT, WE WON'T

Overview

We Will, We Might, We Won't is a great tool for prioritising, in a simple way, either current or potential activities and mapping them to highlight how many activities are being undertaken at the same time, or what might need to wait in order to manage the workload.

The tool is circular in format, rather like a mandala (a mandala is a complex abstract design that is usually circular in form. Mandala is a Sanskrit word that means 'circle'), and is similar to the Who's Here? tool (Tool 4). One can also divide the circle into segments, which may represent time periods, such as business periods (e.g., Q1, Q2 etc.).

Because the 'We Will' activities rest together in the middle of the circle this will give a sense of how much work might be undertaken at the same time, which could highlight questions about time or resources.

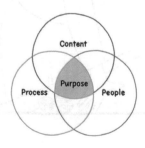

The Meeting Kaleidoscope

Being able to extract all the content in order to create a full and complete picture of activity is important for this tool to work well and add practical value to the group.

Flow flavour

1. Prepare your chart, preferably using a large piece of paper as the circular model will take up space. Draw one central circle with enough space to hold sufficient sticky notes and another circle around it, again with space between the two. If you need to segment the circle add in your straight lines as required. Finally add your headings, using the example illustration as a guide.
2. Invite participants to, individually, write the title of each activity on a sticky note, using one sticky note per activity.
3. Once all participants have written their activities on their sticky notes, invite them to place the sticky notes in the appropriate area of the chart. It doesn't matter at this stage if there is duplication. Sticky notes placed on the central 'We Will' circle denote activities that *must* be undertaken. Sticky notes placed on the 'We Might' circle represent activities that are important but may not represent an urgent priority, or they could be delegated to others. Finally, sticky notes placed outside the circle indicate activities that are not adding value and could be stopped.
4. Focus the group initially on the central circle when all sticky notes have been placed on the chart (removing duplication as you go). Encourage a discussion about what this means for the participants in terms of (1) how many activities have been identified and (2) what this means for implementation or collaboration. How realistic might implementing all these activities be? What does this mean for how the group works together? What activities might need to be 'pushed out' to 'We Might' in order to achieve the important tasks?

5. Allow the group time to consider the central items in turn, and decide on whether they either remain or are moved out of the central circle.
6. Next, move to the second circle and follow the same process, considering each activity and whether it needs action or can be delegated or 'pushed out' to the 'We Won't' area as something that does not require the group's focus. Under what circumstances might an item placed in this second area move into the middle?
7. Finally, consider the activities placed outside the second circle. You don't need to spend a lot of time on this but do ensure you give time to at least acknowledge if there are any differences of view.
8. If the chart has been segmented into quarters, for example, invite the group to review the proposed timeline and check if this is achievable, and move sticky notes as appropriate.
9. At this stage you should have a whole picture of activity, indicating what's important and what's not.

Watch out!

It is possible that you might have a lot of sticky notes posted on the chart. Using smaller sticky notes for this tool will help as participants simply need to add the activity title, and maybe their initials if appropriate.

Resources and kit

A large sheet of paper, large compass, smaller sticky notes, marker pens (fine nib for writing on smaller sticky notes), ruler/straight edge and tape.

Catherine's expert insight

'This tool can be used as an effective way of assessing what's going on for a group in terms of workload. It can help a group to effectively "trim the fat" and discover where energy and resource is being duplicated or wasted. To get the *most* value from it, and to use it to aid more strategic conversation and meaningful planning, taking time up front to define the goals and aims of the group will mean that the conversation becomes far more than a data-gathering exercise.'

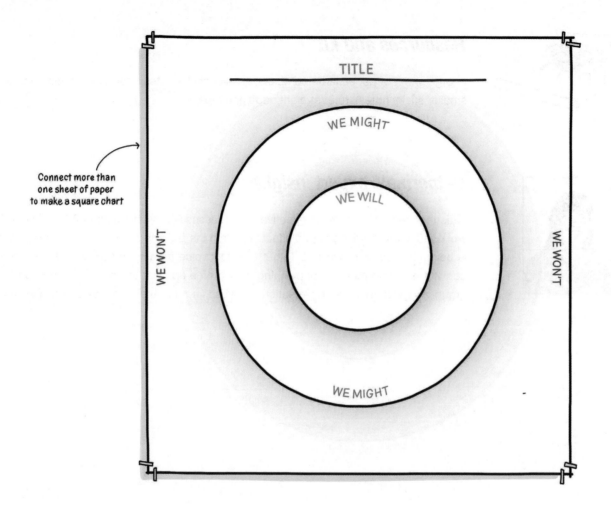

Connect more than
one sheet of paper
to make a square chart

TITLE

WE MIGHT

WE WILL

WE MIGHT

WE WON'T

WE WON'T

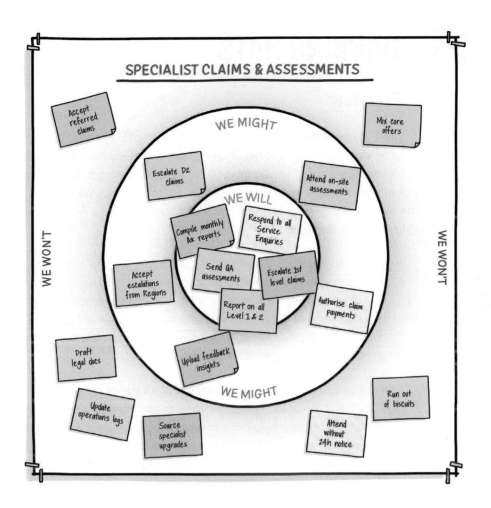

[33] THINKING HATS

Overview

The Thinking Hats tool originates from the work of Edward de Bono in the mid-1980s. The idea underlying the concept of the Thinking Hats is that we have the capacity to think in a number of different ways and, if we structure these ways of thinking in a sequence, we are able to approach and work through tasks and issues. De Bono identifies six different ways of thinking, each of which encourages our brains to perceive a topic or subject from a distinctly different perspective. In summary, these are:

- Managing (Blue Hat) – what is the goal we wish to achieve?
- Information (White Hat) – what are the facts, and what information is available to us?
- Emotion (Red Hat) – what is our gut reaction or emotions we associate with this goal?
- Discernment (Black Hat) – what reasons do we have to be cautious about this goal?
- Optimistic (Yellow Hat) – what are the benefits we will enjoy by achieving this goal?
- Creativity (Green Hat) – what else is possible?

A key benefit of this approach is that all participants are encouraged to think in the same way together, which reduces the complexities arising from participants thinking in different ways at the same time. I have added this tool here as it can be used in decision making; however this tool could equally sit within the Stretching stage of a successful meeting. The process below illustrates a simple decision-making process. De Bono suggests further combinations of working through the Thinking Hats (e.g., problem solving, identifying solutions) depending upon your requirements.

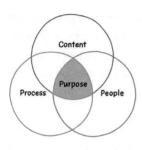

The Meeting Kaleidoscope

Process is very important here, especially how long the group remains at each 'Thinking Hat'. Naturally the content will flow when the process is managed well.

Flow flavour

1. Prepare your six charts and arrange them equally around the room or in a row along a wall if you have space. Feel free to draw any type of hat for each poster, as long as the colour matches the process.
2. Explain the purpose of the process, for example to review a specific issue or idea and test it from several different perspectives of thinking.
3. Start with the Blue chart. The group may have already agreed the topic to be discussed. If this is not the case, ensure the whole group understands the topic being reviewed and summarise this in writing on the chart.
4. Move to the White chart. Encourage the group to consider the facts about the topic. What do we know to be true? What information do we have to support our thinking? This stage is not about judgement, and you may need to guide the group to avoid applying opinions. Remain with the White chart long enough to ensure the facts are sufficiently captured (e.g., 10–15 minutes maximum).
5. Move to the Green chart but spend a short amount of time here, no more than 5 minutes. Invite the group to share any creative thinking they have about the topic. For example, could the goal be achieved differently?

6. Move to the Yellow chart. Invite participants to share what's positive about the goal. What are the reasons to be happy about this plan? What are the benefits to be enjoyed? Again, capture these on the chart. Spend a maximum of 5 minutes on the Yellow chart.
7. Move to the Black chart. Draw out any reasons participants might have to be cautious about the goal. What might get in the way of achieving the goal? Spend a maximum of 5 minutes on the Black chart.
8. Move to the Red chart. What emotions are the group experiencing, however positive or negative? Avoid applying judgement here, as this is simply about what emotions are being experienced rather than why. Spend a maximum of 2–3 minutes here.
9. Finally, move back to the Blue chart. Given what we now know about this goal, having considered it from different perspectives, what decision will the group make about whether to proceed with the goal, or not?
10. If you have other topics to explore using this process, do so, and compare the results for each.

Watch out!

- Spending a short amount of time in each 'hat' area is key, although it is appropriate to spend longer at the White chart due to the facts that might need to be discussed in detail.
- For this process to work well all participants need to be in the identical 'thinking mode'. Carefully guide any participants who might wish to return to a particular chart once it has been discussed.
- Signpost that time at each chart will be short, and the group need to think swiftly and state what's on their minds.

Resources and kit

A large sheet of paper, marker pens and tape.

Catherine's expert insight

'This process can also be used to prepare individual thinking before a meeting, or even used alone as a tool to aid thinking. Introducing a group or individual to the Thinking Hats concept and then providing them with a visual template to note their thoughts about a topic from the perspective of the six different hats encourages broader, deeper thought and leads to a considered conversation. Some people may notice that they more readily think from the perspective of one hat over another. Developing more flexibility in their thinking and growing their ability to look at issues and ideas from different hat perspectives can be seen as a core skill, essential when needing to satisfy multiple stakeholders or solve complex problems.'

What's your goal?

What are the facts?

What's our gut reaction?

Why should we be cautious?

What are the benefits?

What else is possible?

What's your goal?

We are moving to a new HQ

What are the facts?

- Move will take place in week 8
- New HQ is 5km west of current location
- New space has been allocated to us
- New space is fully open plan
- Meeting room space on floor 4
- Hot desking will be in place
- Paperless office system will be implemented

What's our gut reaction?

- Anxious about change
- Excited about change
- Great to start afresh – energised
- Need reassurance that it will work

Why should we be curious?

- This might disrupt our normal service during the move
- Do we need to get rid of records and paperwork?
- Not everyone will like the new desk plan
- Access to meeting room space might be difficult
- It will take longer to travel to work

What are the benefits?

- This is a great new start in a new office
- Opportunity for new ways of working
- Much nicer environment in which to work
- Will lead to more face-to-face communication
- Hot desking will mean we see different colleagues
- Closer to shops and the park!
- New restaurant and coffee bar

What else is possible?

- We can't change it but we have the gift of making this what we want it to be.
- Let go of assumptions of who should sit near to whom
- Let's start right from a blank page

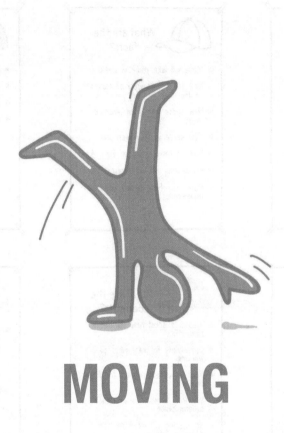

MOVING

[34] NEEDS AND OFFERS

Overview

There is a common saying that 'the answer is in the room'. The success of many decisions made in the meeting will rely largely upon the capability of the participants to make it happen, either themselves or through others. Participants may be unaware of the skills and expertise each other offers, but if they did know they would most certainly seek support from each other when there is a skill or knowledge gap rather than looking elsewhere for a solution.

The purpose of Needs and Offers is to highlight the skills and knowledge each participant holds (relevant to the meeting content and actions agreed) which may be of value to the whole group. The tool and resulting conversation will encourage greater levels of collaboration and mutual support within the group, leading to delivery against agreed actions.

The Meeting Kaleidoscope

The content being generated is hugely important here so that participants can see the potential in what's being offered and needed. There's no doubt that this is also about people, and mutually supporting each other to achieve the collective goal.

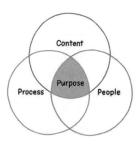

Flow flavour

1. Prepare a basic chart using the example illustration for inspiration. If you can, use paper large enough so that there is plenty of space for both needs and offers as you may have a lot of sticky notes placed on the chart.
2. Invite participants to use their sticky notes to write down what they offer to other participants, and what they need. This could be anything from sharing expertise and knowledge, to physical resources. Most importantly everyone must commit to supporting each other to fulfil these needs after the meeting – within an agreed timescale.
3. Participants should add one offer or need per sticky note, and place them on the correct side of the chart.
4. Encourage participants to add their initials to each of their sticky notes, as this will make it easier to remember who is offering or needing support and follow up afterwards.
5. Once all the sticky notes have been added to the chart, invite participants to review the needs and offers on the chart. If they are able to respond to another participant's need they should remove the sticky note and keep it. Conversely if someone has offered something they need they should remove that too. Allow approximately 10 minutes for everyone to get what they need.
6. Not all offers and needs may be removed. Return to the sticky notes, especially in the needs category, and check whether anyone can help to fulfil these needs. If this is not possible ask the group to briefly suggest who may be able to help. Draw the group's attention to any remaining offers.
7. Ask participants to retain their sticky notes and commit to following up with each other within the agreed timescale.

Watch out!

- Be mindful of those needs that may be left on the chart at the end of the process. The people who have offered them may be unhappy that their needs have been unmet.
- Ask yourself what you can do as meeting leader to encourage a conversation about who can help, so that everyone feels supported.

Resources and kit

A flipchart, marker pens, sticky notes and tape.

Ben's expert insight

'Meetings are one-off forums that will always be in the moment and are often short-term focussed but should be seen as part of something much bigger. In the medium term they may be important to the development of a team or the lifecycle of a project, whilst in the long term will play a huge part in change and the cultural fabric of an organisation.

I like to use this Visual Tool when working with groups who are coming together as part of a piece of work as it helps them to understand how they might work together collaboratively to land the goals, what they can learn from others, how they can lean on others and what their role is within that group.'

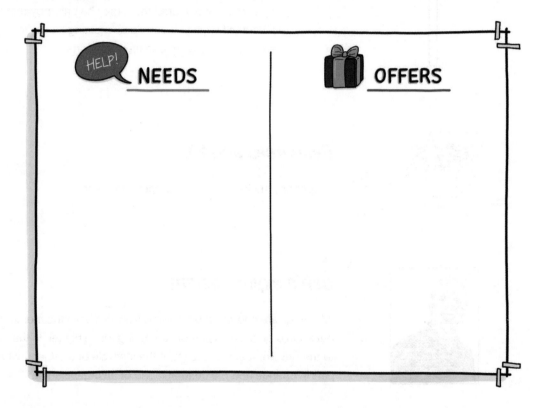

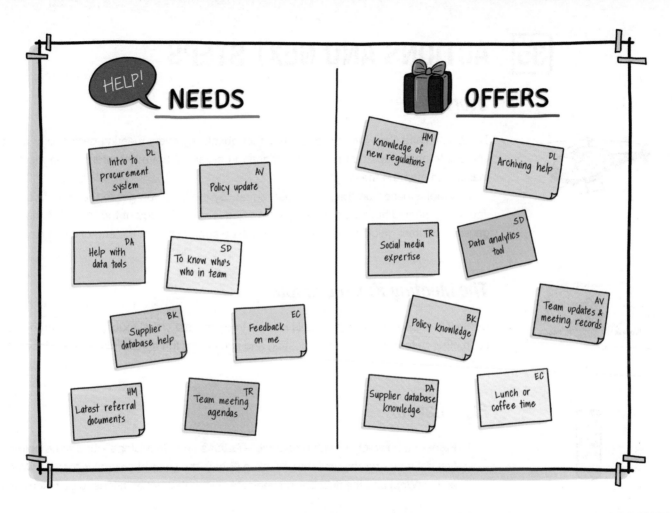

ACTIONS AND NEXT STEPS

Overview

The Actions and Next Steps tool is a must for absolutely every meeting designed to capture the immediate next steps that must be actioned in order for the momentum in the meeting to be maintained after the meeting.

This tool is based on the reliable list format. By the time you get to the end of your meeting your group should have well and truly converged. The advantage of the list is that the group can generate content quickly and easily, which will be appreciated at the end of a busy meeting.

The Meeting Kaleidoscope

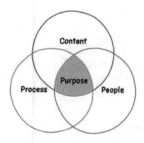

Content is super-critical here, as this is likely to be the last visual touchpoint the group have with each other before they leave the meeting and implement the agreed plans. Make it count!

Flow flavour

1. Prepare a basic chart with a heading – Actions and Next Steps – and three columns. The first column is for the action to be taken (What), the second column is for who will take that action (Who) and the final column indicates when that action needs to be taken (By When).

2. Explain the tool format and lead the group in a conversation about the immediate actions that need to be taken following today's meeting. You may wish to capture the information yourself or ask a member of the group to do that for you.
3. Before moving to the next point on the list, ensure you have clearly captured the content for all three columns.
4. Continue until all the key actions have been captured. Encourage participants named on the chart to take a photo of the chart so they have an immediate reference point.

Watch out!

This tool is not about capturing all the detail of activities identified in the meeting itself. Ensure the group understands that this tool is for the actions that need to happen straightaway to make the big plans happen.

Resources and kit

A flipchart, marker pens, ruler/straight edge and tape. Cameras for participants.

Helen's expert insight

'I find it helpful to introduce this chart at the start of the meeting and encourage the group to complete it throughout the session. In this way you can keep track of decisions and actions as they happen (whilst they are fresh in everyone's mind). Then, towards the end of the meeting, you can recap the list and re-affirm commitments.'

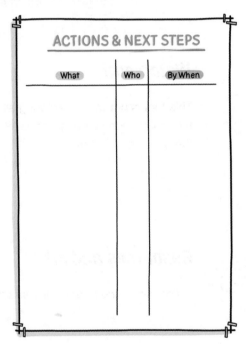

ACTIONS & NEXT STEPS

What	Who	By When
Take photos of all charts	All	Before we leave
Arrange next meeting	Tony	By end of this week
Send invites to Abi and Tess (with clear purpose and outcomes)	Dan	By end of next week
Update team web page	Vernon	By end of week 34
Update reporting templates	Angela	By end of week 34
Provide new concept brief to this team for feedback	Chan Wai	By end of week 35
Feedback to Chan Wai on concept new brief	All	By end of week 36
Brief leadership team on progress to date	Minh	At next Leadership Meeting – check with Ellie's PA for next date.

36 | MY BEST ADVICE

Overview

The purpose of My Best Advice is to provide a powerful way of finishing a meeting, especially when participants might benefit from a little encouragement and motivation from each other, for example when there is a big project to deliver together.

The tool often works best with smaller groups, especially if you want everyone to hear each other's advice; however you can make this work in larger groups as participants can share their advice with each other in smaller groups.

The impact of this tool depends very much upon the framing you give as meeting leader. The more positive and energetic you can be the better. Remember to frame the question in the context of the meeting purpose, outcomes and what has been agreed in the meeting. The advice participants give to each other will be most powerful when it is specific and grounded in the meeting content, rather than being generic in nature.

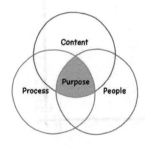

The Meeting Kaleidoscope

Unsurprisingly this tool is about people supporting and helping each other. A super way of ending on a motivating high.

Flow flavour

1. Provide all participants with a marker pen and blank sheet of paper. Photocopying paper will be perfect.
2. On a flipchart, pose the question to the group. For example: 'What's the one piece of powerful advice you give to this group right now?' It will be helpful if you have prepared this chart in advance. Encourage participants to be punchy and concise.
3. Allow participants a few minutes to reflect on the question and write their advice clearly on their sheet of paper, using one side only. Although text is essential, they could add emojis for a little extra character.
4. Once everyone has written down their advice, ask someone to share their advice with the group. Encourage others to do the same. If you are leading a large group, encourage participants to form smaller groups and share together.
5. Try taking a photo of the group together, each holding their sheets so they can be clearly seen. This could make a powerful image to share in your post-meeting documentation.

Watch out!

There aren't many ways you can go wrong with this tool. Try to avoid the infamous 'creeping death' by encouraging anyone to speak next, therefore avoiding the tendency to 'go around the table'.

Resources and kit

Plain paper, such as photocopying paper, and marker pens.

Helen's expert insight

'It can be tempting (and quite natural) for individuals to be more concerned about the way they will share their advice than to truly listen to the advice of others. As you set this session up, ask the group to focus particularly on the advice of others and leave a few seconds in between each offer to let the last piece of advice sink in. You could support this with a quote from Nancy Kline's book *Time to Think*: "The quality of your attention determines the quality of other people's thinking."'

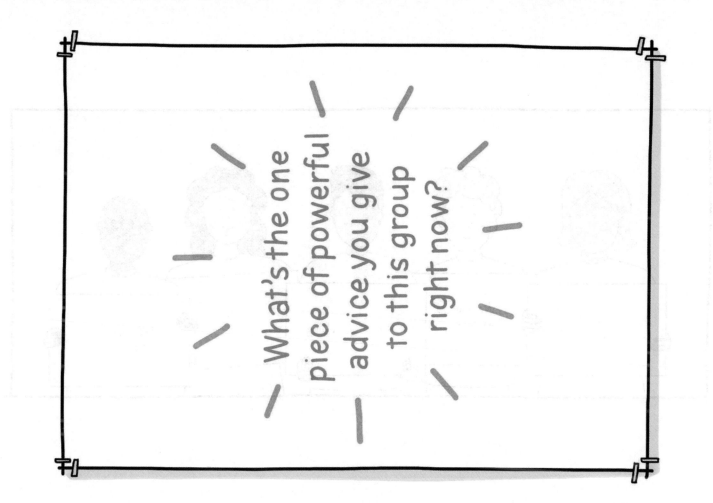

What's the one piece of powerful advice you give to this group right now?

37 WHAT'S OUR STORY?

Overview

For many critical meetings there are often others (who weren't in the meeting itself) who are waiting to know the outcome and what will happen next. The purpose of What's Our Story? is to encourage participants to be aligned on the 'story' they will tell about the meeting, so that everyone conveys consistent messages. It is easy to assume that, because everyone has been in the same meeting together, everyone has heard the same thing and will communicate the same message. Not necessarily so.

The Meeting Kaleidoscope

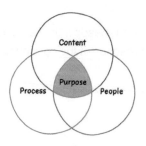

The story generated will contain critical content for the group to go out and create a 'line of one' for consistent communication.

Flow flavour

1. Prepare your flipchart template using the example illustration for inspiration. You may wish to use more than one flipchart if appropriate. At the least you should have a space for the big headline, and another for the key sub-headings to add further context.

2. Explain the purpose of the conversation to the group, and either lead them through the conversation or allow the group to self-organise, including someone who will capture the key points on the chart as the conversation progresses.
3. Allow enough time for the group to identify and agree the key headline and points. A suggestion is 10 minutes to keep the conversation focussed.
4. Once the group have concluded their conversation encourage them to stand back and absorb the information. Seek clarification that everyone is in agreement.
5. Encourage participants to photograph the chart so they have the information ready as soon as they leave the meeting.

Watch out!

- A big caution for this tool is not to get bogged down in the words used for the headline and key messages, as the purpose of this tool is to identify the essence of the communication points and not to deeply wordsmith.
- Remember that participants will add their own style when communicating the messages onwards.

Resources and kit

A flipchart, marker pens and tape. Cameras for participants.

Ben's expert insight

'I love this tool and use it regularly. Often outputs from the meeting will need to be worked on and developed into branded documents to be shared and circulated – but that doesn't stop the stakeholders, your teams and partners wanting to know how it went and what's changed.

Getting this defined in the meeting, agreement and commitment from everyone in that meeting to share the same messages is a hugely powerful thing. It fosters engagement and alignment, stops any whispers and rumours, and manages expectations.

In my eyes, every meeting should have an agreed, core story which is proactively used to communicate with all stakeholders.'

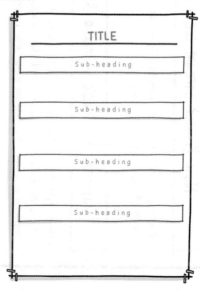

WEEK 13 MANAGEMENT MEETING

New Project Stream Gets Green Light

- Anne confirms a 'go' to proceed to second stage with budget allocated.
- Becks to lead planning team.

Intranet Feedback – mixed AND constructive

- High quantity of feedback – 70% response.
- Mixed opinions received on what has worked well.
- Sam to ask for cross-team input into making improvements.

Office Refurb is on the Horizon

- Great opportunity for us to input into new style space.
- James to lead on our team's input to what's required. More news in Week 15.

All Staff Conference Date Confirmed

- All Staff Conference on 1st September.
- A project team is needed for initial planning day on 8th April (let Adela know if you would like to be involved.)
- We will have a stand in the Marketplace this year!

38 | LETTER TO ME

Overview

Letter to Me is a wonderfully personal tool that allows each participant to express themselves in their own personal way without being concerned about what others may think. By writing a letter to themselves dated in the future (e.g., in six months' time) each participant has the opportunity to commit wholeheartedly to what will be achieved by that point.

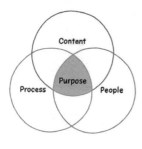

The Meeting Kaleidoscope

A personal process that strongly aligns individual aspirations to succeed with a focus on commitment to act.

Flow flavour

1. Provide each participant with a sheet of paper (photocopying paper will be ideal), an envelope and a pen.
2. Explain the purpose of the process, which is to write a letter to themselves explaining all the great things that have been achieved, relevant to the plans agreed in the meeting. The letters should be positive and specific in describing the positive impact that the actions led

to, and must be written as if they are going to be opened on a specific date. Make sure everyone knows the date when the envelopes will be opened.

3. Allow participants an appropriate amount of time to write their letter. Inevitably they will need time to think about their letter before committing pen to paper. Between 20 and 30 minutes should be sufficient.

4. Once written, invite each participant to place the letter in the envelope, seal and write their name on the front. They should then give this letter to you.

5. Organise for the letters to be returned to the participants on the agreed date. This may require you to retain the letters or to pass to someone who can re-distribute the letters. When the letters are opened participants will have the chance to read their letters and reflect on what has really been achieved since they wrote their letter.

Watch out!

- Avoid giving too little time for participants to write their letters. Hurried letters will not provide the tangible benefit needed.
- If you are not retaining the letters yourself, aim to ask someone who will be perceived as independent from the group, and who will remember to return the letters promptly on the right date.

Resources and kit

Paper sheets (e.g., photocopying paper), sealable envelopes and writing pens (e.g., biros).

Helen's expert insight

'It is surprising how often people write a letter to their future self and forget to include themselves in it! As humans we can be all too willing to describe a wonderful picture of success in great detail but forget to paint ourselves into that picture. The result is a descriptive piece of writing without a real personal connection.

A Letter to Me works best when it is fully associated with the author. Take a look at the example and you'll see!'

39 ACTIVITY PLAN

Overview

Whereas the Actions and Next Steps tool (Tool 35) focusses on the immediate actions following the meeting, the Activity Plan is much more detailed and captures the details of actions as activity streams over a period of time.

I have used the Activity Plan many times with diverse groups and I have found its primary beauty to be how it combines what might otherwise be disparate strands of activity into one place. If silo working is a challenge you experience in your organisation, this tool can support an effort to align teams and foster collaboration.

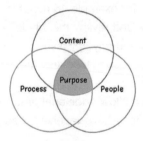

The Meeting Kaleidoscope

Content, content, content. Copious amounts of tangible inputs and outputs being utilised here.

Flow flavour

1. Prepare your chart, using a large sheet of paper. The example illustration illustrates a timeline (using vertical lines) and several horizontal streams to indicate streams of activity.

2. At the right-hand side of your chart, write in the vision or goal the group is looking to achieve. This will act as a constant reminder of the target.

3. Explain the process to your group, and suggest that the group splits into sub-groups to focus on each of the different horizontal streams. It will be beneficial for the teams to be as mixed as possible so that a holistic view is available in each group.

4. Allow the groups to identify the activities that need to be undertaken for their stream within the relevant timescale. Activities should be written on sticky notes with a clear and concise description of the activity (the 'what') and the initials of the person (or name of team) who will lead that activity (the 'who'). Where the sticky note is placed on the timeline will indicate the 'when'. If they need clarity from another group on a specific point encourage them to ask questions and seek out the information. A Knowledge Zone (Tool 12) might also be hugely useful.

5. The groups may need plenty of time to plot their activities, for example 45 minutes. After the initial period encourage the whole group to stand back and review the whole activity plan. Invite each group to summarise their stream, highlighting any key issues they have encountered. Encourage the remaining participants to ask questions for clarity and provide feedback.

6. Once all sub-groups have summarised their activity stream allow additional time for the groups to work on their streams based on the feedback they have received. I suggest approximately half of the time used for the initial work.

7. Invite the whole group to review together a second time, identifying any remaining conflicts or complexities that need working out. Once these are resolved you have a high-level activity plan ready to be worked into a detailed project plan should this be required.

Watch out!

- A group standing around a chart on a wall can be crowded. This is when placing a chart on the table can be ideal, allowing the groups to stand around the chart and see everything.
- Ensure there is clarity on who will undertake each activity. Don't be afraid to continue asking the question if names/departments are not placed against activities, as an action plan without clarity on who will deliver is unlikely to gain traction later. Be mindful of participants nominating others for activities, especially if the nominated person or department is not in the room. Enquire as to how they will seek agreement from others to get involved in the work to be done.

Resources and kit

A large sheet of paper, ruler/straight edge, marker pens, sticky notes and tape.

Catherine's expert insight

'Be patient, be firm, keep focussed and be prepared for ebbs and flows in the group's energy and enthusiasm. Action planning is the real deal! It's where people have to make genuine commitments and consider the impact that what they say will have on their future working experience.

As such there is a lot of thinking going on and when people are thinking hard most of them become quieter. Don't be afraid of silence. It's a sign something is happening. If it becomes apparent that a part of the plan is not getting completed be genuine in your observation. Highlight it and ask the group if you are right and why that might be. The conversation that follows will unlock the group or will surface bigger conversations that need to be had. Better to know that there is an issue with an area of the plan than to get fake commitment and no action!'

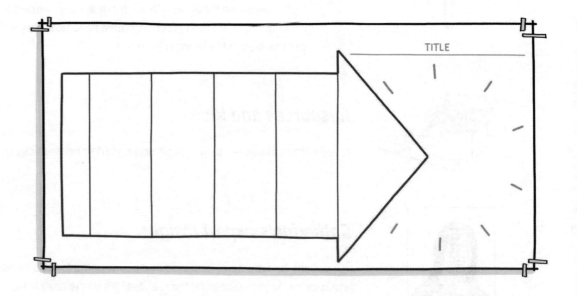

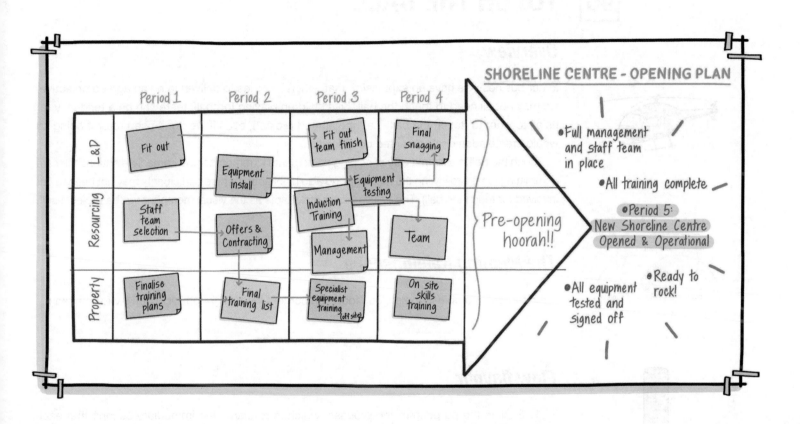

40 | TOUCH THE BALL

Overview

In our business we have an expression that, when it comes to delivering on an agreed objective, we may not all need to touch the ball. Like children playing football, there can be a tendency for us all to want to 'touch the ball' (i.e., the agreed project), even If we don't need to or if doing so would create additional unwanted complexity.

Touch the Ball is a simple way of helping participants to remember the immediate actions they are committing to take following the meeting, and also highlighting where participants may not need to get involved (or touch the ball). The ball, in this context, acts as the visual metaphor for the project itself.

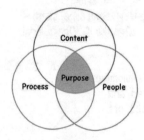

The Meeting Kaleidoscope

A fun tool that combines the serious focus on content with a light physical activity for the team.

Flow flavour

1. Explain the purpose of the process, which is to clarify the immediate actions that each participant needs to take in order to fulfil their commitment following the meeting.

2. Taking the ball, throw it lightly to a participant. The participant with the ball summarises the actions they need to take following the meeting. If they miss an action, the group has an opportunity to remind them of the action, which they can note down immediately. The ball is then thrown to another participant and the process is repeated until all participants have explained their actions or noted down any they had forgotten.
3. Should a participant catch the ball, but not need to be involved in the project/activity, they should clearly state 'I don't need to touch this ball' so that everyone can hear it. This will help them to remember that they need not be involved.

Watch out!

- Ideally, use a large soft (e.g., foam) ball. Always be mindful of safety!
- You're at the end of your meeting and energy may be a little lower. Encouraging participants to stand up during this process will get the blood flowing and creates a more assertive and powerful finish.

Resources and kit

A large, soft ball. Participants will also need their own note pads and writing pens to ensure they have noted their actions.

Catherine's expert insight

'This tool can effectively surface underlying issues within a team. It certainly makes visible the work that needs to be done. In doing so it can also flush out over-dependency on individuals, unequal pressure being put on different members of the team and the conscious or unconscious exclusion of team members. As such it can be used both to tie up the loose ends for a team and to analyse what's going on and provoke conversation and exploration. If physical space makes working with an actual ball difficult then drawing the touchpoints onto a poster of a ball is a useful second best.'

WHAT JUST HAPPENED? EVEN MEETING SUPERHEROES NEED TO REFLECT

I am hoping that, by the time you have an opportunity to get to this section of the book, you will have used a number of the tools in Section 6 in your meetings, and with huge impact!

The life of a great meeting leader is a busy one. In fact the more effective your meetings are, the more likely you are to be asked to plan and lead more of the same. In many ways it's a nice problem to have.

TAKE TIME TO REFLECT

Whilst it might sound appealing, 'saving the world' one meeting at a time, the time one takes to reflect on 'what just happened' can often be squeezed or wiped out completely. The result is that any important learnings and observations about one's meetings and the tools used are kept in one's head for a short whilst and then lost in the melee of business.

The Meet with Impact Reflection Tool is designed to give you the space to record your insights and reflections after your meetings. I strongly encourage you to note your thoughts immediately after your meeting so that memories are fresh and useful. You might also wish to consider seeking feedback from your meeting participants.

In addition to the meeting title, purpose and participants, there is space to record the tools you used, which you will also have captured on the Meet with Impact Planner. Space has been given to what worked well, which could include aspects of your own facilitation, the response of the group, and the decisions reached. Finally, please take time to consider what you would wish for if you were to run the meeting all over again. What might you do differently next time, and how can you implement that learning for next time?

If you take a copy of one of the blank pages for noting your thoughts, you can keep it with your planner for future reference, or why not download the free PDF from our website (read on for details).

I sincerely wish you every success as you lead ever more impactful visual meetings, making those inspired and subtle twists and turns of the kaleidoscope.

THE MEET WITH IMPACT REFLECTION TOOL

MEET WITH IMPACT REFLECTION TOOL

Meeting Title:	Face to Face ☐ Virtual ☐

Meeting Purpose:

PARTICIPANTS:	TOOLS:
WHAT WORKED WELL:	I WISH:

© 2019 The Facilitation Partnership Limited

MEET WITH IMPACT REFLECTION TOOL

Meeting Title:	Face to Face ☐ Virtual ☐

Meeting Purpose:

PARTICIPANTS:	TOOLS:
WHAT WORKED WELL:	**I WISH:**

MEET WITH IMPACT REFLECTION TOOL

Meeting Title:	Face to Face ☐ Virtual ☐

Meeting Purpose:

PARTICIPANTS:	TOOLS:
WHAT WORKED WELL:	I WISH:

MEET WITH IMPACT REFLECTION TOOL

Meeting Title:		Face to Face ☐ Virtual ☐

Meeting Purpose:

PARTICIPANTS:	TOOLS:
WHAT WORKED WELL:	I WISH:

MEET WITH IMPACT REFLECTION TOOL

Meeting Title: | | Face to Face ☐ Virtual ☐

Meeting Purpose:

PARTICIPANTS:

TOOLS:

WHAT WORKED WELL:

I WISH:

YOUR FREE MEET WITH IMPACT PLANNER AND REFLECTION TOOL

For your free PDF copy of the Meet with Impact Planner and the Reflection Tool to print and use time and time again, visit our website – www.thefacilitationpartnership.com or www.inkythinking.com – and look for Meet with Impact.

SOURCES/BIBLIOGRAPHY

- *5th Discipline Fieldbook: Strategies for Building a Learning Organization*. Peter Senge et al. 1994. Nicholas Brealey Publishing.
- *Black Box Thinking: Marginal Gains and the Secrets of High Performance*. Matthew Syed. 2016. John Murray.
- *Coaching for Performance: The Principles and Practice of Coaching and Leadership*. John Whitmore. 2017. Nicholas Brealey Publishing.
- *The Facilitator's Guide to Participatory Decision Making*. Sam Kaner. 2007. Jossey-Bass.
- *Fierce Conversations: Achieving Success in Work and in Life, One Conversation at a Time*. Susan Scott. 2003. Piatkus.
- *Humans Are Visual Creatures. Tea Romih. 2016. Seyens Educational Institute.*
- *The Knowledge Creating Company: How Japanese Companies Create the Dynamics of Innovation*. Ikujiro Nonaka and Hirotaka Takeuchi. 1995. Oxford University Press.
- *The Medici Effect: What Elephants and Epidemics Can Teach Us About Innovation*. Frans Johansson. 2017. Harvard Business Review Press.
- *The Meeting Book*. Helen Chapman. 2016. LID Publishing.
- *Out of the Ashes: Business Continuity Management Lessons from Iceland's Volcanic Eruption.* Roberta Witty et al. 2010. Gartner.
- *Six Thinking Hats*. Edward de Bono. 2016. Penguin Life.
- *The Social Life of Information*. John Seely Brown and Paul Duguid. 2017. Harvard Business Review Press.
- *Visual Meetings: How Graphics, Sticky Notes and Idea Mapping Can Transform Group Productivity*. David Sibbet. 2010. John Wiley & Sons.
- *Virtual working – it is possible to be truly engaged?*. Nigel Purse. 2018. thehrdirector.com

INDEX

2 by 2 138, 268–72
3 Word Introduction 136, 159–62
5 Whys 138, 263–6

accessible information 41
action 29
Actions and Next Steps 139, 300–3
  and Different Perspectives 254
Activity Plan 139, 317–21
address labels 106
agenda
  PREP 147
  vs process 66–7

sharing before and during virtual meetings 96
anticipation 27

balanced information 39–40
Blanket 37
board tables 123–4
body language 83, 85
Bomber 37
Boston Matrix 268–72
Brailsford, Dave 14
BRAVE information choices 39–42
Brown, John Seely 32, 33, 35
bullet tip marker pens 108

bullets 113
Buzan, Tony 191

cameras 106
  see also photographs
Captain Instant 37
car parks 122
case, lower vs upper 117
CEO's personality, taken on by organisation 36
chalk pastels 108
change 10–13
  to meeting culture 38–42
  small details 14–15
  visibility 15

Chapman, Helen 50
chisel tip marker pens 108–9
circles, drawing 107, 109
closing down the meeting space 120
Clustering 137, 174–8
Collaboration Continuum 67–8
colour, use of 104, 111–12
commitment 29
communication 58
  after virtual meetings 99
compasses 107
competitive advantage 17
confusion in virtual meetings 86

content of meetings 57–8
 tools 136–9
continuity 166
cost-effectiveness, virtual
 meetings 82
cross-cultural working 28
cross-talk in virtual meetings
 86

data *see* information
de Bono, Edward 288
Deciding stage of meeting 74,
 75
 tools 138, 267–93
designing visual resources
 102
Different Perspectives 138,
 253–7
directional ideas 61
distraction element of virtual
 meetings 87
diversity 60–4
 Different Perspectives 253
 virtual meetings 84

drawing
 bullets 113
 circles 107, 109
 Collaboration Continuum 68
 shapes 114–15
 straight lines 107, 109
Duguid, Paul 32, 33, 35

Einstein, Albert 265
e-mail
 invitations to meetings
  55–6, 132
 lists, virtual meetings 93
energising information 42
engagement 26–7
Enhanced Idea 138, 249–52
 and Different Perspectives
  253
environmental influences 7
Essence of... 136, 156–8
expectations 27
eyelines, in virtual
 meetings 88
Eyjafjallajökull 78–80

facilitators of virtual meetings
 91, 95
first followers 13
Five Whys 138, 263–6
flexible working 81
flipcharts 104
 drawing on 109–10,
  113–15
 virtual meetings 93, 97–8
 writing on 111–12, 115–18
flow of meetings 69–72
fonts 112
forgiveness vs permission 16
format 3
framing 3
 negative 4
 positive 4, 8, 16, 18

Gartner 80
Gives and Gets 136, 168–72
Graffiti Wall 137, 179–82
grids 68
groan zone 71–2
 GROW 220

Why? Why? Why? Why?
 Why? 263, 264
group think 279
GROW 137, 219–23

Hammer 38
Helped and Hindered 136,
 163–7
hidden nature of virtual meetings 85
history 30
 Timeline 209–13
Hoarder 38
Human Cluster 137, 224–7

ideas, directional vs intersectional 61
impact 9–10
In Our Dreams 138, 248–62
inclusion 60
 virtual meetings 84
information
 accessible 41
 balanced 39–40

benefits 31–2
defined 34
energising 42
Knowledge Zone 187–90
participants, focus on 43
relevant 40
social nature 32–4
understanding 34–5
versatile 41–2
virtual meetings 84, 96, 99
insight advantages, virtual
    meetings 83
Inspiration Filter 137, 214–18
intersectional ideas 61
invitations to meetings 55–6
e-mail 55–6, 132
iPads 121
Iraq war 70
'It's easy, what you do is...'
    137, 183–6

Japanese organisations,
    knowledge creation 17
Johansson, Frans 61

Journey/Transition Map 138,
    229–33

kaleidoscopes 48–9
Kaner, Sam 69–72, 263
Kline, Nancy 306
knowledge
    creation 17
    explicit 17
    sharing 16–17
    tacit 17
Knowledge Zone 137, 187–90
    and Activity Plan 318
    board table 124
    and GROW 221
    and Inspiration Filter 215
Knox, Vicesimus 32–3, 81

Letter to Me 139, 313–16
lists, and use of colour 112
lone shirtless dancing guy
    13–14
loud participants, virtual
    meetings 86

marker pens 104–5
    colours 104, 111–12
    using 108–10
Maverick 36
Meet with Impact Planner 120,
    130–5
Meet with Impact Reflection
    Tool 327–32
meeting culture 8, 36–8
    changing 38–42
    in your organisation 44–5
Meeting Kaleidoscope 49–50
    content 57–8
    people 58–66
    process 66–8
    purpose 50–6, 58, 62–3
    tools 127, 136
    visual information 94
meeting scenarios 22–5
    invitations 55–6
meetings
    defined 18
    flow 69–72
    stages see stages of
        meetings

virtual see virtual meetings
milestones in meetings 30
Mind Map 137, 191–5
    tablets 121
Moving stage of meeting 74,
    75
    tools 139, 294–324
Mugshot 136, 149–51
My Best Advice 139, 304–8

need for meetings 6
Needs and Offers 139, 295–9
noisiness, virtual meetings 85
Nonaka, Ikujiro 17
non-verbal behaviour 83, 85

Opening stage of meeting 73,
    74, 75
    Meet with Impact Planner
        130
    tools 136, 140–72
organisational characteristics
    10–12
    size 12–13

organisational culture 7
  CEO's personality 36
  cross-cultural working 28
organisational purpose 51–4,
  62–3, 146
orientating participants in
  virtual meetings 97

pacing of virtual meetings 98
paper rolls 104
participants
  focus on 43
  Meet with Impact Planner
  130
  see also people
participation 26–7
pastels 108
peer pressure 279
pens see marker pens
people
  diversity 60–4
  inclusion 60
  Meeting Kaleidoscope
  58–66
  tools 136–9

see also participants
permission vs forgiveness 16
PEST 137, 196–9
photographs
  cameras 106
  Different Perspectives 255
  The Essence of... 157
  My Best Advice 305
  virtual meetings 93, 97–8
  visual working 29
Picture Cards 138, 244–8
planning see preparation
portability, virtual meetings 83
PowerPoint presentations 189
PREP 15, 136, 144–8
  and Inspiration Filter 216
preparation 119–20
  Meet with Impact Planner
  120, 130–5
process 66–8
  Meet with Impact Planner
  130
  tools 136–9
Process Map 137, 200–3
  and Enhanced Idea 250

prohibitive nature of virtual
  meetings 85
punctuality in virtual meetings
  87
purpose
  Meet with Impact Planner 130
  of meetings 50–6, 58, 62–3
  organisational 51–4, 62–3,
  146
Push and Pull 138, 234–8

quiet participants, virtual
  meetings 85

reflection 326
  Meet with Impact Reflection
  Tool 327–32
relevant information 40
reports, simplicity 97
resources see toolkit
rudeness in virtual meetings 87
rulers 107

safety advantages, virtual
  meetings 84

Schwarzkopf, Norman, Jr. 70
scribe 118
Senge, Peter 67
setting up for meetings 120
sham consultation 68
shapes 114–15
Show Me the Money! 138,
  277–81
  and Inspiration Filter 215
simplicity in virtual meetings
  97
slide decks 120–1
  Collaboration Continuum 68
  orientating participants 97
  PowerPoint presentations
  189
  simplicity 97
sloppiness in virtual meetings
  87
small details 14–15
social nature of information
  32–4
soft pastels 108
speed advantages, virtual
  meetings 82

stages of meetings 73–5
   Meet with Impact Planner
     130
   tools 126, 136–9
sticky dots 107
sticky notes 105
straight edges 107
straight lines
   drawing 107, 109
   writing in 117–18
Stretching stage of meeting
   73, 74
   tools 138, 228–66
SWOT 137, 204–8

tablets 121
Takeuchi, Hirotaka 17
tape 106
Team Sky 14
technology
   board tables 123
   glitches 85
   slide decks 120, 121
   tablets 121
   see also virtual meetings

templates 98
The Essence of... 136, 156–8
'There is never any milk!' 138,
   239–43
Thinking Hats 138, 288–93
Three Word Introduction 136,
   159–62
time advantages, virtual
   meetings 83
Timeline 137, 209–13
timings 130, 132
toolkit 128
   contents 103–8
Touch the Ball 139, 322–4
Tripp and Tyler 88
Two by Two 138, 268–72

urgency, tyranny of 68–72

versatile information 41–2
virtual meetings 79–82
   agreeing ways of working
     92
   breaking into groups
     99–100

capturing ways of working
   93
   challenges 90–1
   disadvantages 85–8
   facilitators 91, 95
   insights 88–90
   tips 95–9
   tools 136–9
   visual information 94
virtual working 81
   benefits 82–4
visibility
   change 15
   virtual meetings 82
Visual Voting 138, 273–6
   and Enhanced Idea 250
   and Inspiration Filter 215
   and 'There is never any
     milk!' 240
visual working, reasons for
   25–9
voting dots 107

waff 119
'We are here' (PEST) 137,

196–9
We Will, We Might, We Won't
   138, 282–7
What's Our Story? 139,
   309–12
white address labels 106
Whitmore, Sir John 219
Who's Here? 136, 152–5
Why? Why? Why? Why?
   Why? 138, 263–6
Working stage of meeting 73,
   74, 75
   tools 137, 173–227
writing
   colour, use of 111
   fonts 112
   lower vs upper case 117
   in the moment 115–18
   scribe 118
   see also marker pens

You are Welcome! 136, 141–3